A KIND OF MAGIC

A KIND OF MAGIC

Mollie Harris

Illustrated by John Ward, R.A.

CHATTO & WINDUS · LONDON

Published by
Chatto & Windus Ltd
42 William IV Street
London W.C.2

*

Clarke, Irwin & Co. Ltd.
Toronto

First published September 1969
Second Impression September 1969
Third Impression November 1969
Fourth Impression June 1974

ISBN 0 7011 1450 9

Printed and bound in Great Britain by
Redwood Burn Limited
Trowbridge & Esher

To my grandsons
PETER LEIGH & JONATHAN
with love

CONTENTS

Introduction

I have called my book *A Kind of Magic* because to
me my childhood was a time of magic. I don't mean
'the rabbit in the hat', fairy-godmother-trans-
formation sort, but simple experiences and moments that can be recollected and looked at time
and time again—treasured, unforgettable, irreplace-
able happenings that I have tried to record here.

There was a sense of wonderment about our
everyday lives—searching for the first wild flowers
of the season—sliding on a frozen pond at night in
the crisp, frosty air—the magic of staying with my
grandparents—luscious, country, stuffingy, Christmas smells—home-made jam boiling on an open
fire—the magic of firelight and stories at bedtime—
breviting over the fields, wooding and mushrooming—the kindness and good humour of neighbours
and friends in those hard-up, happy times—the
closeness of a big family in an overcrowded but
happy home—our mother's indestructible gaiety
and sense of wonderment—some of which, thankfully, rubbed off onto her children.

The Village

WHEN I look back, the days of my childhood seem to have had a kind of magic about them. They were colourful, exciting, demanding days, full of wonder and discovery, joy and adventure.

The village where we lived was set in the low-lying valley of the Windrush—it was long and straggly, stretching a mile and a half from the milkman's in Little Ducklington to the flour mill cottages in Ducklington proper. It seemed always to smell of cows—a sweet, grassy, pungent smell, a mixture of milk, warm animals and manure.

Apart from the ordinary cottages there were several farms dotted about—Pudney Wilsdon's, Hoppy Druce's (Hoppy because of his bad foot), Holtoms' and Stranges'. Good-living and hard-working, they employed a number of local men, mostly who lived with their families in tied cottages near the farms. Men who were known by their calling—Carter Temple, Shepherd Spindlow, Carter Porter, Cowman Godfrey—names they were known by all their lives, and nobody thought of addressing them any differently.

Men who didn't work on the farms in Ducklington puffed up to Witney on their bicycles to the blanket mills. Most of the ordinary girls worked on the looms at one or other of the blanket factories, too, often walking over 'The Moors', a short cut to the town; few could afford a push-bike. The more genteel girls served in the shops and in-betweens worked in the big steam laundry. But a few still went away to domestic service.

Most of the cottages in the village were built of Cotswold stone, roofed with grey stone slates quarried at Stonesfield near by. Others were thatched in deep thick yellow thatch that seemed almost to touch the ground. And the long gardens at the backs were filled with cabbages, potatoes, rabbit hutches, pigsties and earth closets.

A few houses of red brick were dotted about. The flour mill, too, was red-bricked, and its continuously throbbing engine, chunk, chunk, chunk, could be heard all over the other end of the village.

The heart of our small community was the wide square, dotted with cottages, near the church, close-knit and protecting. Over the road was the school and pond.

There was a chapel up the other end, as well as two pubs and two small shops—these were in the front rooms of cottages, their tiny windows bursting with glass jars of brightly coloured sweets, sherbet dabs, liquorice pipes, and aniseed balls—a haven for a child with a penny to spend. There was Baker Collis to bake our bread, and the milkman who came clanking up the path in his hobnailed boots to dole out milk from a shiny can.

We had travelling men who came puffing down the dusty road. One weekly visitor was Hog Puddin' Walker, a giant of a man who pedalled his hog puddings—black and white puddings—and beautifully plaited chitterlings, in a yellow wicker basket fixed on the front of his huge black bicycle. His wares were kept covered with a whiter-than-white cloth, and there was always fresh green parsley dotted about among the puddings.

Saturday was something of a field day for us— that was when Benny Clements, the oil and rag and bone man, paid us a visit. He was small and ragged and wore a long overcoat winter and summer; it reached nearly down to the ground, almost covering his boots. He brought paraffin oil right up to the doors of the cottages. Amongst his rags and rabbit skins were tall shiny tins of sweets. 'Benny's Black-uns' we called them, and for a handful of rags the old man would dole out a few of these black peppermint sweets, although the flavour was often lost be-

cause Benny handled them with black-grimed, paraffin-soaked hands.

Many a duster or house flannel found its way to Benny's cart. 'Yes, you little hounds,' Mother would shout, 'no wonder I can't find a duster anywhere—halfway to Witney on Benny's cart, I'll be bound!'

We called another tradesman 'Spetter' King, because he spat on his hands a lot, although some people said he was called this because he stuttered. Whatever the reason was it didn't matter. All we were interested in were his sweets. In his shop in the town near by he made a wonderful assortment of boiled sweets, clove, lemon, aniseed and cinnamon, acid drops and peppermints. And once a week he would cycle out to the village to try and sell some. We would hang round him, a dozen or more of us.

'Giss one, giss one,' a big boy would say.

'Du—du you want to to buy any?' Spetter would splutter.

'How du we know if we shall like 'um? We ain't tried 'um yet,' another would say.

And we would nudge each other, pressing forward till we nearly knocked Spetter over, and his bike and his wares as well. Then he would give us each a sweet to taste, popping them into our open pink mouths like a parent bird feeding a brood of young fledglings. Perhaps one of the boys would buy a ha'p'th; then he would slink off with half a dozen more kids following him saying, 'giss a lick, giss a lick', knowing darn well they would never be given a whole sweet.

Packmen called too; sometimes our mother bought thick, warm, twill sheets and boots for us all, paying perhaps a shilling a week onto the dog-eared card until the debt was cleared. By then the boots were worn out, so more were ordered. With seven growing children skipping and scauting about it must have been boots, boots, nothing but boots to pay for on that dog-eared card.

Tramps and gypsies were other visitors; tramps always called on us, the middle cottage in a row of three. It was funny they never called at the others that stood either side of us. Our mother said that the tramps left signs for their fellow travellers by scratching marks on the wall with bits of stone. We would search the walls for signs but never found any. But whatever time of day it was our mother never turned a tramp away with an empty billycan. Gypsies she wasn't too fond of—they used to cadge water from our well, dipping their dirty buckets down into the depths of the cool spring water, sometimes breaking the well hook into the bargain.

When it was the annual feast several families of show people ('Gypoes' we called them), would arrive on 'Chalky', the village green, and because the row where we lived was the nearest to the green, we had to put up with them. They were in and out of the yard all day, bringing hordes of children and dogs with them.

The children would snatch gooseberries from Mrs-next-door's bushes and the dogs would chase cats all over the neatly dug gardens. If you refused them water or grumbled about the kids and dogs they would fling out a string of abuse and curses. The best thing to do was to let them get on with it for a couple of days while the feast lasted. Then they would pack up their stalls and kids into the brightly coloured caravans, harness their ponies, and were away to the next village fair.

A KIND OF MAGIC

The nearness of the close-knit village enveloped us every day. We youngsters and our mothers were a little community on our own; only the men and girls who worked in the town knew a different sort of life. We knew everything that was going on— birth, illness, death were everyday topics—we children knew little of their proper meaning, but talked about them as our elders did.

Always somebody's mother was having a baby— we saw birth and death in the farmyards and fields— but we didn't probe or bother to find out why or where—many of us were thirteen and fourteen before we started to pick up the facts of life, and then these were whispered and giggled to us by other girls a little older who had already started work and had picked up snatches of conversations from people they worked with.

I must have been nearly fourteen when a gang of us stumbled across a village girl and boy lying close in the thick standing grass. 'I'll bet he is giving her a french letter,' a fifteen-year-old girl whispered. But I wondered what this youth could be doing with a french letter—he had only attended the village school. It was as much as any of us could do to master English, let alone read a french letter lying down in a grass field.

Then two of the older girls that I was with started singing and cat-calling to the courting couple:

Down in the meadow
Where the nuts are brown
Petticoats up and trousers down. . . .

they sang. The young man in the grass half-rose and shouted to them, 'Shut up that singing or I'll clout your ears.' 'If the cap fits, wear it,' answered the cheekiest of the girls, and we all ran off squealing and laughing.

At Michaelmas other families moved into the tied cottages, bringing new children to the school, often very shy; probably they had lived miles from anyone, up in the fields somewhere before coming to Ducklington.

One family, the Goodsons, were like this—the Mother was a timid, white-faced person. She made the most lovely chocolate cake—at least I thought it was marvellous. She told me years afterwards that it was only flavoured with cocoa—she did not have the money to buy currants and things.

The pond was just opposite the church and in winter became a meeting place for every able-bodied person. The hard cold frosts of January froze the surface solid. We would spend most of our time sliding there. In the evenings men, women, boys and girls would congregate down there—someone might bring a lantern if there was no moon, and we would cut great long slides from one side of the pond to the other. Dozens of us, tearing along through the frosty night on those glassy slides.

A KIND OF MAGIC

When the thaw set in we were lost for a while—then it was back to the fireside and our stepfather trying hard to get 2LO on our crystal set. 'Be quiet or you'll all go to bed,' he would shout, 'and take that dratted kettle off the fire, I don't know whether it's that or London I can hear.'

On Saturday nights poor people walked up to Witney. After eight o'clock you could buy 'bits': oddments of meat and bones. A shilling's-worth would make a lovely meat pudding or pie, enough for the biggest family. Many of the villagers kept a couple of pigs. One would be killed and salted for the family's use, the other would be sold to pay for the toppings (pig food).

Everybody had big allotments as well as their gardens. Both men and women toiled on these; into the late evenings they would work, growing enough potatoes and other vegetables to last all the year round. Children, too, helped their parents with picking up potatoes, hoeing and weeding. Nobody could afford 'boughten' vegetables or fruit.

This then was how most of the folk managed. 'Rough and enough' the women called the heavy meals they dished up for their families. Some did not have enough to eat, and pale, skinny children either grew up as weaklings or died. But for most of us, we thrived on stews and suet puddings, bread and dripping, home-made jam and fat bacon.

The Family

MY first and most lasting memory of my mother is that of a tall, majestic person. She was five-feet ten, well-built, and with fine features. She had a mop of thick black wavy hair coiled on top of her head and laughing, sparkling eyes, and she was as strong as an ox. Of course, over the years she became grey and bent but the sparkle in her eyes was always there.

She had started her working life at thirteen when she was packed off to service, never earning any more than £8 a year. Of course she had good food in the gentry's houses and uniforms were found.

Then she met and married my father, a mail-van driver. When they set up house their furniture was

20

not the ordinary cottage type, but upholstered chairs and a good sideboard and a really nice bedroom suite. For he was a hardworking, steady fellow and had not squandered his money.

Then just two months before I was born my father died. Our mother already had three children, my two elder brothers, Bern and Bunt, and my sister Betty, and they were all under five years old. Apparently our father, normally a very fit man, had been taken to Oxford Infirmary with acute appendicitis. Within a week it had turned to peritonitis and he died.

Then for our mother the long struggle began. Her parents begged her to go back to their quiet village in the Cotswolds, but she refused, thinking that we would stand a much better chance to get on in life if we stayed where we were. 'A little bit nearer civilization,' as she put it. So with the help of neighbours and friends lending a hand or keeping an eye on us she took a job in the town at the local cinema, The People's Palace.

Her job was to take the money and show customers to their seats, but her generosity was her undoing. She would let old Susie go in free. Susie was a dirty woman who picked up dog-ends and sorted over people's dustbins. She did not want to look at the pictures but just to sleep in the warm cinema. Our mother used to say: 'You go down and sit in the front row Susie, you'll be all right.' The front

seats were the very cheap, hard ones. But Susie,
looking for comfort, used to sneak up to the more
expensive red-plush seats at the back. One night
the house lights went up and there, between a
Colonel and a Major, sat Susie, snoozing. Susie was
banned from The People's Palace and our mother
got the sack.

She did other jobs—one was gloving at home.
Quite a number of the village women did this hand-
stitching of gloves, brought out to them from a local

factory. The work was tedious and very poorly paid and our mother, who always hated sewing, did not do this for any longer than she could help.

At this time we were living in a tiny low-windowed cottage down Hell Corner near the church. One day we children were all crammed by the bedroom window while our mother mopped and dusted and changed the bed. Suddenly there was a knock on the door and four small faces surged forward to see who the caller was. I was first to meet him, straight through the glass panes onto the dirt path below, suffering no more than a badly cut leg. The caller was our future stepfather and he was tall and good-looking, with a mop of curls and bright blue eyes. He was dressed in his army clothes and I could feel the prickly material stinging my legs as I sat on his lap to be comforted. He became a regular visitor, and looked at our mother as I had never seen anyone look at her before.

He was a despatch rider and told us tales about the countries he had been to and brought us presents—serviette rings (which we never used), carved in wood from the Mount of Olives, and a Bible too, with the same fine wood for its covers; a red fez with a black tassel for each of us; and a photo of him taken on a camel and one of him standing with a guide half-way up a Pyramid. From him we heard about places with strange names—Mesopotamia, Dardanelles, and he sang cheeky army songs to us—

and we loved him.

After he married our mother we all moved from Hell Corner to a bigger cottage in Little Ducklington, a small community of thirteen houses separated from Ducklington by the village green. Here, three more children were born, my stepsister Mick, and brothers, Ben and Denis. Our cottage called 'Wayside' was a two-up and two-down affair with a large landing that served as a third bedroom, and it was to be our home until the older ones began to leave and marry—with our parents and seven growing children it must have been crammed, to say the least, but we didn't notice it.

The meals were all cooked and eaten in the living-room, but the washing-up was done in the back kitchen where there was a small larder and a place we called the dungeon. It was really a cupboard under the stairs, where we kept sacks of potatoes in winter time, and the brooms and brushes and things.

Somehow on a great black grate our mother concocted wonderful meals—tasty and filling. In a

great oval pot that was suspended over a good fire
she cooked hunks of fat bacon along with potatoes
and cabbage. The vegetables were put into string
nets to keep them separate. When they were cooked
she would fish them out of the steaming saucepans
with the aid of a fork. Then into the same water and
along with the bacon she would drop a suet pudding,
perhaps a roly-poly or a currant 'spotted dick', and
sometimes just plain suet to be eaten with golden
syrup on it as a special treat.

Occasionally an uncle and aunt who lived in the
Cotswolds would send us a couple of rabbits by
post. They usually came at a particularly hard-up
period. 'If the Lord don't come, he sends,' our
mother would shout gleefully, holding up the furry
objects. In no time at all the skins were pulled off.
Sometimes we would get sixpence for these from
Benny, the old oil man. Then she would make up a
good fire, poking the red coals underneath to heat
the oven which was at the side of the fireplace.
Into the oven went the jointed rabbit covered with
thickly sliced onions and halved potatoes covered in
dripping. And later we would all sit down and have
a meal fit for a king.

In our house jam was made from anything that
was going, and during one bad period for about
three years we almost lived on blackberry and
apple jam. It came out of the jars in great solid
lumps—we had it on porridge, boiled rice, suet

puddings, toast—three times a day sometimes, till we were all sick of the sight of it. But at least it was wholesome and nourishing. Blackberries were ours for the picking, everybody had an apple tree in the garden, and sugar was no more than 2d. a pound.

Once when dried apricots were cheap our mother bought some—soaked them in water till they 'plimmed up' and then set about making jam. It only cost about 3d. a pound to make, but she made one mistake—she cooked it in an iron saucepan. By doing this she killed all the apricot flavour, but we had to eat it. It was much too precious to give to the pigs. We waded through about fourteen pounds of the stuff, and after all these years I still expect apricot jam to taste of iron.

But except for an occasional slip-up like the iron saucepan, most of our mother's cooking, although prepared in a slapdash fashion, was the best I've ever tasted. She never weighed or measured anything.

Sometimes she would buy three penn'orth of bones, set them in water in the oval pot, throw in every sort of vegetable and herb that was available, and top it all up with suet dumplings as big as tennis balls. 'That'll put a good lining in your insides,' she'd say to us as she ladled out the thick, warming stew.

When it began to get dimpsy in the evenings the paraffin lamp was lit and carefully stood in the centre of the table where it cast a soft, gentle light over the room. Through the years, in spite of crowded families in the village, I never did hear of anyone's lamp being knocked over. Candles were used to light the rest of the house.

The only fire scares we ever had was when our mother, perhaps late back from shopping in the town, or just wandering over the fields, would fling paraffin on to the fire to 'jostle it up' ready for cooking. Then there would be a minor explosion and flames and wood ash would shoot out into the living room covering everything, and sometimes setting the chimney on fire as well. 'Quick!' she would shout to one of us, 'fetch me a sack.' She would plunge the sack into a bucket of water and stuff it up the chimney with the end of the broom handle, and quell the fire. When the danger had passed she would fetch the sack down, bringing with it great lumps of black smelly soot. 'Never mind,' she'd cry, 'that'll save me having it swept.'

Washing day, always on a Monday, began before we left for school. First, every drop of water had to be drawn from the well out in the yard. Our mother hooked the bucket onto the long-handled well hook, plunging it down into the cool depths, bending and pulling up the dripping bucket time after time, until she had filled the old washing copper which was built into the corner of the wash-house. It stood away from the cottage and in it we kept our stock of coal, wood, old bikes and tools. When the copper was full she would light a fire underneath to get the water good and hot. All day long she would be washing, blueing and drawing more water. The only aids she used to get the clothes clean was a big bar of yellow washing soap, and soda. A few years later, when Hudson's Washing Powder was put on the market, housewives thought they were really in clover.

In summer our mother would drag a heavy table out from the wash-house and do her work in the sun. Some women in the village had huge wooden roller mangles—not us though—and our mother, the world's worst wringer, often slapped her washing over the line dripping wet. The copper was still hot at the end of the day so she would fill it up again and the next morning the water was quite warm, for Tuesday was the day when the bedroom floors were scrubbed in a mixture of soda water and paraffin. This was done to make sure that there were no fleas hiding in the floorboards, for fleas, like head-lice, were easily picked up.

There were no mats or lino in the bedrooms—such luxury was kept for the living-room only. This was warm and cosy; the stone floor was covered in fawn coconut matting, but by the fire stretched a lovely rag rug, one our parents had made and the sort of thing to be found in most of the cottages. They were made from old coats and dresses. We children used to help cut up the strips of cloth into pieces about six inches long and an inch wide. From somewhere our stepfather would get a good big strong hessian sack which was washed and opened out flat to form the base of the rug.

It was quite simple to do: you just made two small holes in the hessian with a wooden meat skewer and poked a strip of material through, and each time you did this it made a double tuft. You just kept doing row after row until the hessian was covered. The colours used would be mostly browns and black but people usually managed to find a bit of bright material, blue, green or red, to make a little pattern in the centre and the corners.

A KIND OF MAGIC

In the summertime the living-room got very hot, because the fire had to be lit in the afternoons for cooking. But later on, when things were a bit easier, our stepfather brought a paraffin stove and the vegetables were cooked on this.

Then, if on a Sunday we had a joint or a tin of potatoes or a rabbit to be baked, we would take them down to Baker Collis's. In his bread oven he would cook any of the villagers' dinners for a penny. We had to walk to and from the bakehouse with the baking tin, and the lovely smell that rose from it on the return journey was almost unbearable.

But on one day each week in the summer the fire had to be lit specially, so that our mother could do the weekly ironing. As soon as the fire was nice and red she would hang a metal stand onto the fire bars, and the irons were stood on it—the fronts against the fire.

Two irons were necessary, one heating while the other was being used. She used to test the hot irons either by holding them up near her face or by spitting on them—then the little balls of bubbling spit galloped down the iron onto the hearth mat.

Such a lot of ironing there was too: knickers and nightgowns, pinnies and petticoats, working shirts and overalls, as well as bed linen. Then the freshly ironed clothes were hung on the fire-guard to air. Ours was a big oblong one, made of wire mesh with brass round the top. The guard was always kept round the fire when it was alight, so that the little 'uns were safe from it. But when we children had gone to bed our mother used to take it away so that they might get more comfort from the fire.

When we had weeks and weeks of rain the washing had to be dried indoors, either draped round the guard or slung up on lines in the back kitchen where it dripped damp and dismal, fogging up the windows, giving us colds and coughs.

Further down the garden, and quite a walk from the house, were ours and Missus-next-door's lavatories, side by side. These, when we first lived there, were 'privies' or vault type, a huge deep hole in the ground that was emptied about twice a year. Over the top of this hole was built a box-like contraption with two holes or places to sit. This was a 'two holer' and what most villagers had, although some had three and four holers. In ours there was one large hole for grown-ups and a smaller one for children. These really should have had wooden lids on when not in use, but not ours; they had most likely gone up the copper hole years ago.

After we had been living at 'Wayside' for about seven years these awful vaults were replaced by bucket lavatories, but not before an incident happened that could have easily been a tragedy in our family. I must have been about nine at the time and young Ben, one of my stepbrothers, about four. He had got into the habit of wanting to answer nature's call in the evening just as he and Denis were undressed ready for bed. He would say 'Mum, I want to go to the lavatory,' and our mother would say 'Mollie, take him down,' and I, no bigger than two penn'orth of 'apence, would stagger down the dirt path with Ben on my back, our light a candle that often blew out on the way down.

Ben was a cheeky, spoilt show-off, and each night as I carried him down he would jog about on my back and whine, 'I wants tu go on the big seat, I wants tu go on the big seat.' I suppose he thought he was old enough, but of course he was much too small.

As the weeks went by I got fed up with this

nightly ritual, and suddenly, one night, I didn't bother to sit him carefully over the small hole but backed straight on to the big one and let him go. He folded up just like a shut-knife and went down the hole backside first, leaving only his head, hands and feet showing. He let out a blood-curdling scream and I yelled at the top of my voice—the noise brought the whole family running pell-mell down the garden path. They hauled Ben out, smelly and frightened. I got a darned good hiding and Ben a good hot bath. But that 'larned' him. He answered nature's call earlier in the day after that.

Our stepfather, after working for a couple of years on a farm, got a job as a lorry driver for the 'Bewry', the local name for the Brewery in the town. He liked this varied job; it took him to many of the towns and villages within a radius of fifty miles where he delivered great barrels of beer and bottled stout to the firm's pubs and sampled the beer at each one.

At weekends he was glad to do a bit of seasonal work for the farmer who had previously employed him. I've known him take on the job of cutting and laying a hedge just for the privilege of taking the wood home, which was mostly blackthorn that burnt like coal. We kids would help by dragging the piled-up truck home time after time, with the smaller children carrying the chips.

He kept many of the habits he had acquired in the army and he was very strict with us. No going out in the morning without a clean pair of boots and no talking at meal times. If we were disobedient it was 'quick march' up to bed whatever the time of the day. He kept himself as smart as it was possible to do with such a big family, and his military moustache was kept clipped and twirled. He sang a lot too, mostly army songs, sometimes sentimental ones, sometimes cheeky—

> *Put me on a hiland where the girls are few*
> *Put me in a cage with the lions at the zoo.*

This he would sing to the tune of Mendelssohn's 'Spring Song'.

My favourite was—

> *Round the corner behind the tree*
> *Sergeant Major made love to me.*
> *Oh when are you going to marry me?*
> *For I should like to know*
> *'Cos every time I look in your eyes*
> *I feel I want to go*
> *Round the corner behind the tree.*

In his younger days he had emigrated to Canada and would tell us hair-raising stories of that great continent, but he got fed up with the life there and saved to pay his passage home—soon to settle in our quiet village with a ready-made family.

THE FAMILY

Often on a winter's night we would sit at home in the dimpsy light, gazing into the glowing embers and playing a game called 'Pictures in the fire'. Usually it was just the four of us younger ones, Mick, Ben, Denis and myself, curled up on the warm hearthrug. The game was nearly all imagination but such fun to play.

'Look,' Mick would shout. 'Look, there's a fairy castle like the one in my Christmas picture book.'

'No it isn't,' Ben would butt in. 'It's an army fort with turrets and guns coming out of it.'

'It's not either, it's just like Windsor Castle where our King and Queen live,' I told them seriously.

While we were arguing, the picture would change as the coal and wood burnt away in the shiny black grate. Now the castle became a man's bearded face —a bit like Brummy Edwards. Now it was a dog. 'Our dog,' Denis the youngest would cry. And for a moment a dog's head, his mouth open as if barking, would glow clearly in the fire. Now it became a bird—its fine etched wings outstretched—and then, as if by magic, it changed to a lovely lady, her hair piled high, her dress full and flounced.

Suddenly the door was flung open and a wave of cold air would sweep round the room as Bern, Bunt and our stepfather came in from work, cold and hungry. Our mother would jump up, 'Time I lit the lamp,' she'd say. 'Didn't realise the time had got on so, listening to you kids.' And in a moment the warm glow of the oil lamp filled the room. You could still see pictures in the fire, but they never seemed quite so vivid and real as they had seemed in the almost darkened room.

'Come on,' my brothers would say, 'move back a bit you kids, we bin out at work all day.' Stiff, hard boots would be taken off and stood in the fender so that they might be warm and dry to put on in the morning.

Our mother would dish up the cooked meal, serving the menfolk first; then we children had ours, dipping chunks of bread into the gravy or thick stew.

'Jam roly-poly for pudding,' our mother would

cry, brandishing a great knife, 'whose turn is it for the end bit?'

'Our Mollie's,' came a chorus. 'No it isn't, it's our Bern's,' I would protest. Arguments followed and excuses were made; nobody wanted the end bit, there was never any jam in that piece anyhow.

'You can wash up in here tonight, you girls,' our mother would say if the weather was cold. I would fetch the enamelled bowl from the freezing back kitchen and an old tin tray to turn the crocks on to drain. Mick was supposed to dry up. But she often invented a surprise trip to the lavatory or a bad hand or headache, cunningly getting out of her stint.

I would try to slip the kettle back empty on the hob. Someone would notice. 'Come off it Mollie, go and fill it up.' Nine times out of ten I'll bet the bucket was empty, so it was out into the ice-covered yard to the well, thrusting the well hook, simply freezing, and slippery with ice, down into the depths. The stars in the clear sky were sparkling and crackling in the frosty air as I drew up the heavy, full bucket.

Then it was off to bed for all of us children, so that the grown-ups might have a little warmth and comfort. Sometimes we might be allowed to stay up a bit late if one of the neighbours brought in their gramophone, and we would sing to the accompaniment of the singer on the scratchy records. But mostly we went to bed much earlier than lots of the village children. Our mother said it was good for us and that we grew while we were sleeping anyhow.

But sometimes when she was feeling tender and sentimental she would tell us stories of the past. Of

how, when she was a schoolgirl, she used to have to go up to the big house every night during the winter-time to get jugs of rabbit soup. This was during the late 1800's, when times were very hard and in some places people were starving. Not in their village though. Thousands of rabbits were shot on the estate and made into stew in the great kitchens of the big house, and anyone from the village could go and get some daily.

'That stew,' our mother would say, with a far-away look in her eyes, 'was the best I've ever tasted. It was supposed to be for my Dad's tea, but walking back across the park with that lovely smell wafting round my nostrils was too much. I kept having a swig, it was nearly always half gone by the time I got home.'

And another tale she never tired of telling was the romantic one of our great-grandfather, and we children never got tired of hearing it. A dreamy look would steal over her face when she told us:

'Years and years ago your forbears lived in a little village called Preston in Gloucestershire. They were well-off farming people, and lords of the manor at one time. They had three sons, bold, black-haired and good-looking they were too. All over six-feet tall and as strong as the oxen that pulled the ploughs at a nearby farm.

'Job, the eldest of the three, was wild and wilful and a charmer—charm the hindleg off a donkey if he wanted to. When he was about twenty he fell head-over-heels in love with Emily, the pretty daughter of the shepherd who worked on his father's farm.

'What a good-looking pair they made too, he tall

and dark and she a fair, shy little thing. At first they met quite openly, then Job's father got to hear about it. 'Course the fat was in the fire then. There was a most awful row and he dared his son never to speak to poor Emily again. "No son of mine is going to marry a shepherd's daughter," he said.

'Then the couple began to meet on the sly. Job would make any excuse to go out in the evenings, down to see if the cattle were all right or over to the blacksmith's to get the plough mended, just so that he could see Emily for a few moments.

'And do you know what happened then?' Mother would ask us as we sat spellbound listening to her —'they ran away and got married. After a little while the money ran out and they returned to the farmhouse at Preston to find the door closed against them for ever. My Grandfather never had a penny of the family fortune.

'And that,' Mother would add a bit sadly, 'is why we are so darned hard up. But at least you are all big and strong and healthy, and that's something you inherited from him.

'Then there's your own Gramp,' she went on, 'he'll never have a penny to bless himself with— give his head away if he could get it off. Now your Granny, she's different, good job she is else we should never have had a stick of furniture in the house, he'd give it away to anybody. And although we never had any of the family money officially, your Great-Grandfather's younger brother, Sam Broad, saw to it that your Gran wasn't entirely penniless and he helped her no end secretly. He had a business in London besides the farm at Preston.

'Then suddenly it all ended. One day when Sam had been up to London on business, and most likely had a lot of money on him, he boarded the train to come home but he never reached there. All sorts of enquiries were made and at last the police came to the conclusion that he had been set upon and robbed, then murdered, and his body thrown out at some lonely spot. Anyhow nothing was ever heard of Sam Broad again, and the link with us and the rest of the family was broken.'

Some years ago I took my mother back to the little village of Preston and we searched the overgrown churchyard and found tombstones erected to our farming forbears.

One old fellow there told us that when he was a boy the names of some of the Broads were clearly marked on stone slabs in the aisle, but he added 'They be either all worn away or bin took up when they done some building alterations yer a few years back.'

There was a Time

MY idea of heaven was to go and stay at the home of my grandparents who lived in one of those lodge houses on the outskirts of a lord's country estate in a little village in Gloucestershire. My Grandfather was shepherd for this lord and my Grandmother was gate opener, for the lodge where they lived was situated at the main gate that led to the great house that had as many windows as days in the year.

That was how my grandparents met—in the big house. My Gran was head cook there and one of my Grandfather's weekly jobs was to kill a sheep and

44

take it to the great kitchen where it was basted and baked, steamed and boiled for both the gentry and the dozens of servants that were employed there. By the time I came along my grandparents must have been in their late sixties but were still both at work.

The lodge was a sort of bungalow with one large living-room, kitchen, back scullery and two bed-rooms. The one that I slept in was filled with the smell of ripe apples and lavender. Under the bed were boxes and boxes of apples carefully packed away for winter use, and the cool clean sheets that I slept in seemed filled with the scent of a summer garden.

They were great gardeners, both of them; more than half their living came from the well-kept plot. All summer long we picked and potted, pickled and chutneyed anything that was possible to preserve for the coming winter. Such crops they grew! Giant cabbages and potatoes, row upon row of broad beans and peas, such as I have never seen since. My Grandfather liked to eat his broad beans old: 'pitch-eyed' he called them. 'As big as a baby's ear—six on a fork, that's how I like 'um,' he would say, 'an' boiled in a drop of bacon water too.'

Still, they had most everything at their advantage to grow good stuff: a couple of pigs in the sty, and the midden—the useful countryman's compost heap where both kitchen and garden waste was thrown— gave them a good supply of manure.

As well as this there were the yearly 'sheep dags' that formed part of my Grandfather's perks. About a month before the sheep shearing, the flock had to be tidied up a bit, because mucky fleeces were not accepted at the wool staplers. So on a mild spring day my Gramp would round up the sheep, driving a few at a time into a smaller pen, where he would proceed to cut off wool that had become messy at the animal's rear end. For this work he used a pair of hand shears.

Sheep's wool is impregnated with lanolin and this, along with the clinging manure, makes a wonderful base in which to plant kidney beans, and the wool holds the moisture in the roots. It was a job to keep insects off the growing kidney beans and Gramp believed that soot was the best deterrent. But soot is harmful unless it is at least a year old, so it was carefully kept dry and left to mature before they sprinkled it liberally over the young plants.

My Gran and I would sit for hours, stringing and salting the beans for winter use, packing them tightly into fat yellow stone jars.

Another thing my Grandfather believed in was ' 'Tater 'Awks' as he called them. Living on the edge of a great park, their garden was at the mercy of hordes of woodland birds, and the only thing that scared them away was ' 'Tater Awks'. Each spring he would say, 'I shall have to get old Nathan (the head keeper on the estate) to shoot I a sparrow-'awk or two.'

Then he would get several nobbly potatoes—
they had to be nobbly so that he could tie a piece of
string round them. The largest feathers from the
sparrow-hawks were stuck into the potatoes. Then
these feathered contraptions were hung on a piece
of string about a yard long and tied on to a stick
which was pushed into the soil at a slight angle,
leaving the ' 'Tater 'Awk' swinging and twirling at
the slightest breeze. The finest bird scarer I've ever
seen.

Any vegetables and fruit that were not wanted for
immediate use, or for pickling and jam, were used
to make home-made wine. Both my Gran and
Gramp made all sorts which they imagined cured
any complaint.

The gallons of agrimony that my Grandfather

consumed! He really believed that this wine kept him free from rheumatism—most likely it did for he was out on the Cotswold hills for the best part of sixty years in all winds and weathers, with never a day off for illness. Each wine, they believed, had its own medicinal properties; clover for bronchitis, parsley for clearing the blood, beetroot for anaemia, mulled elderberry to sweat out a cold, dandelion for a sluggish liver and metheglin, made from honey and sweet herbs, for a real good pick-me-up.

In the back scullery there was always wine of some sort or another fermenting. Gleanings from the garden and the hedgerows and fields filled the floor of the stone-flagged scullery. Sometimes my Gran and I would go off on a drowsy summer afternoon to gather dandelions and agrimony, burnet and clover.

She never hurried her wines; after boiling they were allowed to settle in a big red earthenware pan. Then she would place a slice of barm-covered toast on top, leaving the concoction to ferment and bubble before straining it off into bottles and casks.

Several journeys I made during the summer to Northleach—three miles there and three back—to get a penn'orth of barm from the local brewery. I was given a two-pound stone jam-jar to collect it in and on the way back I often poked my fingers into the barm, sniffing and savouring the sharp beery taste.

We drank wine after the midday meal and again before going to bed and if anyone called they were always asked, 'Will you have a glass of wine?' At seven years old I was quite a confirmed wine drinker!

I like to think that some of the wine-making, pickling and chutneying that was so very much part of my youth has rubbed off from my Grandmother onto me, and the urge to rush out and pick dandelions and cowslips, elderberries and sloes and transform them into sparkling, brain-tickling wine is most compelling.

My grandparents' flower garden was a riot of colour whenever I saw it, full up with pansies and pinks, stocks and hollyhocks. Old-fashioned sweet briar roses and phlox tumbled and bloomed everywhere. Seeds were carefully gathered and saved each year and cuttings and slips swapped with other villagers.

Visitors never went away unless they were armed with some of my Gran's best blooms. She would scratch and bob about amongst the greenery like an old hen selecting the choicest flowers for them. 'Never give a bunch of flowers away unless you slips a sprig of rosemary in, my dear,' she once told me. 'It'll bring the receiver good luck, and bad to you if you forgets.'

I must have been a favourite grandchild because I was the only one of our family that was allowed to stay with her for any length of time. Although once, I remember, someone drove my mother, Bern, Bunt, Betty and myself all the way to Sherborne to visit our grandparents. We went in a pony and trap and all I remember of the journey is that it was perishing cold and that the driver had piled hay on the floor of the trap—up to our knees it came. This was to help keep us warm during the long ride.

We must have stayed at the lodge overnight because I vividly remember we kids slept four in a bed, a single one at that—my sister and I at the top and our brothers at the bottom, with our feet meeting in the middle.

And the next day we had a scrumptious lamb-tail pie for dinner, something we had never even heard of before. My sister got quite distressed because our Gramp kept telling us that he 'bit 'um off' the young lambs, but it made no difference to either my brothers' or to my ever-eager appetite.

THERE WAS A TIME

For our return journey our Gran packed us up one of her special apple cakes. It had brown sugar and cinnamon sprinkled on the top which gave it a sort of sweet crackly crust. We stopped to eat some and to give the pony a rest at a place called Worsham Bottom where a ghost named Black Stockings is still supposed to run across the road.

It was beginning to get dimpsy and we were scared stiff; owls were hooting and great black bats skimmed over our heads. A stoat ran out of the grass as the pony cropped for a moment and my sister let out a blood-curdling scream and clung to our mother. Bern and Bunt would have liked to have stayed there longer but we others were eager to get moving again.

I loved visiting my grandparents. I used to travel by the carrier's cart part of the way and then get a lift from the baker or butcher to get to the lodge. There was no other way, no railway for miles and miles, and it was 1928 before the motor coaches started to operate between Oxford and Cheltenham. (The lodge is on the now very busy A40.)

A Cotswold Christmas

SUCH excitement there was in our house one Christmas—well, at least for me—for I was getting ready to go and stay with my beloved Gran and Gramp, just for the festive season. At six o'clock in the morning I'd got my flannel nightgown and my pinny packed, and all the little presents we had been busy making for me to take to the grandparents.

Our mother bundled the two youngest, Ben and Denis, into the pram and we set off for Witney where I was to be put in the capable hands of Mr. Groves, the carrier. I was wearing one of my sister's coats that was miles too long and it flapped round my legs as I skipped alongside my mother. She had knitted me an emerald green tammy with a fluffy bobble on, and my stepfather had made me a muff from a rabbit's skin that he had cured. It was cold and frosty and I snuggled my hands deep inside the warm muff, my new shiny boots squeaking in rhythm as we hurried along.

A COTSWOLD CHRISTMAS

I'd been to Sherborne by carrier cart several times before, but never had it been so crowded as it was on this day. The inside was stacked high with boxes and bundles and sacks of apples, and there were hares and rabbits hung on the sides, and some chickens in a crate at the back.

It took the carrier ages to get to Burford because he had to call at several of the cottages in the villages that lay along the valley of the Windrush, delivering boxes of groceries and things.

There were two women travelling in the cart and we chattered and laughed and stamped our feet in the hay that had been put on the floor to help keep our feet warm. I told them where I was going and all about my grandparents. Round, red-faced country women they were and they sat opposite, listening to me. 'You be a mighty fine story-teller,' one of them said. 'Never met a child with such an imagination before. 'Ow old did you say you was—seven? My Nellie's going on fer nine an' 'er can't chatter like you can.'

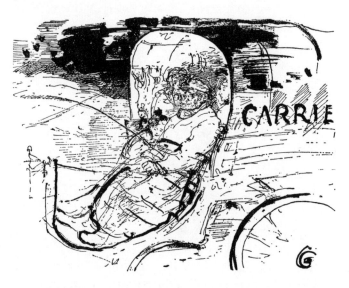

When they got down from the cart at Asthall one called back to Mr. Groves, 'You 'ang on and I'll bring 'e out a hot drink, you'll both be froze to the marrow betime you gets to Burford.' She brought out hot cocoa and great hunks of bread and fat bacon, and it was lovely.

When Mr. Groves went into the cottages to deliver things I could hear squealing and laughing and he would come out red-faced and beaming. Then I noticed that he'd got a piece of mistletoe tucked into the peak of his cap. 'What have you got that in there for?' I asked him, and he threw back his head and laughed a big, throaty, hearty laugh. 'Comes in very 'andy, do that bit of mistletoe,' he replied. But it was years before I realised how handy it must have been.

When we got nearer to Burford Mr. Groves said that I could come out front with him. It was freezing cold and getting dimpsy. He flung a smelly horse rug over my legs. Then, hearing some children carol singing, he started, booming out in his rich voice 'Good King Wenceslas', and I joined in. Even his pony seemed to trot along better for our carolling.

The lamps and candles had been lit in the cottages and Mr. Groves kept banging his hands across his chest to warm them. Then he lit the lamps on the cart and they glowed warm and bright, and as the pony's feet hit the stony road they sent out a shower of sparks like the sparklers did on bonfire night.

We dropped down the last hill into Burford—the lights of the town winking and blinking in the gathering gloom. Mr. Groves pulled up outside a house and lifted me from the cart—I could hardly walk, my feet and legs were so cold. This was where he lived and we went into the hot, welcoming kitchen. His wife sat by the roaring fire making toast for our tea. They had four or five children, merry curly-headed kids they were too. After tea we sat up at the table and made paper-chains to decorate the room with. We cut strips of paper from brightly coloured tea packets, sticking the ends together with home-made flour paste.

About six o'clock Mr. Greig, the baker, called for me. He was to take me on the last few miles to Sherborne. He lifted me up the front of his high cart and wrapped me in a couple of thick coarse flour sacks. He had to deliver bread at three more villages before we got to my Gran's. I was so tired, I'd been travelling since twelve o'clock, and I kept dropping off to sleep, but woke with a start every time the baker shouted, 'Whoa there, Jinny!' to his pony.

Then he brought me out a cup of hot, home-made wine from one of the cottages; it smelt sweet and strong. I took a sip. 'Go on,' he said, 'open your shoulders and let it down, it'll do you good. It just bin hotted with a hot poker.' I could feel the red liquid dropping into my stomach and soon a muzzy feeling crept over me; it was much stronger wine than my Gran's.

Next thing I knew, my Gramp was carrying me into the warm kitchen. My Gran took off my shiny new boots, and my long black stockings, and I cried as the life gradually came back into my frozen limbs. 'Yer Harry,' my Gramp said to the baker, ' 'ave a jackety 'tater, warms yer 'ands an' fills yer belly, that's what 'ot 'taters does.' My Gran cut open a steaming potato for me and spread it with home-cured lard. After a bit the baker got up to leave and my Gran handed him a bottle of 'me matheglum wine' as she called it, and my Gramp gave him a hen pheasant, one of a pair that his employer had given him for Christmas.

Presently my Gran said 'Come on my little maid, you must be tired out—time you went to bed.'

My Gramp swung me up in his great arms— 'Have you put that hot brick in the bed, Mother?' he called. And I was slipped into the lavender-smelling sheets. The heat from the brick that had been in the fire oven all day warmed me through and I was soon asleep.

Next morning when I woke, the pale sun was shining on the window. There had been a sharp frost overnight and the panes were covered with frosty forests of Christmas trees, that seemed to glisten with a million fairy lights. I sat up in bed and scratched the frost with my finger-nail, then huffed on the pane, making a small clearing.

This was the day before Christmas and my Gran had lots to do. I knelt up in a chair by the big white scrubbed table and helped her to prepare the herbs for the stuffing—parsley and thyme, sage and onion. Gleanings from a summer garden they were. After picking and carefully drying the sage, parsley and thyme, she had rubbed the fine leaves from the stalks, afterwards storing the leaves in jam jars tied down with brown paper. The onions came from a big thick rope that hung out in the back kitchen. Roping them had been Gramp's job after he had harvested them the previous autumn, and as we chopped and mixed the herbs together the kitchen was filled with lovely, country, stuffingy smells.

We were going to have such a dinner on Christmas day—that's all we talked about as we plucked the feathers from the bright cock pheasant. I'd never tasted pheasant before—not that my Gran and Gramp had it often, only when his employer, the old squire, presented each of his workmen with a brace at Christmas-time.

My Gran showed me what she had had from her ladyship. 'Look, my dear,' she said, holding up yards of red flannel. 'Make me some good warm petticoats—needs a bit of wool round yer bones in this climate.' There was a pound of tea too, in grey-coloured packets with pictures on them, showing black men and women working in the fields. 'That's where the tea comes from,' my Gran told me. 'Hundreds and hundreds of miles away where it's ever so hot. So hot that the sun turns everybody black.'

Every housewife whose husband worked on the estate had had a present of some red flannel and tea, as well as boots for the children who were still at home.

Every now and then, my Gran had to leave what she was doing and go and open the park gate to let people through to the big house. 'Drat the visitors,' she'd say after several interruptions. 'Don't give a body time to settle at nothing.'

My Gramp came home from work about five o'clock. He was a giant of a man and he wore trousers that squeaked as he walked. He had leather straps round his legs, just below the knees. They were used to hitch the trousers up so that the bottoms would not get wet and muddy. All farm workers seemed to wear them. His face was the colour of a russet apple and he had a mop of black curly hair which he washed every day, and screwed-up, bright blue eyes. I asked why he screwed his eyes up and he said, 'Ah! against that pesky old wind out there,' nodding in the direction of the hills.

A KIND OF MAGIC

There was no trouble to get me off to bed that night. My Gramp said that he would be sure to see that the fire was out before he came to bed so that Father Christmas wouldn't burn himself when he came down the chimney. Hopefully I hung one of Gran's black stockings on the brass bed knob. Yet I wondered how Father Christmas would know that I was not still at Ducklington.

Next morning, almost before it was light, I crawled to the bottom of the bed. He had been. I could feel the nobbly, filled stocking. It was packed with things—sugar-mice, a liquorice pipe, nuts, an orange and a rosy apple, a painting book, a chocolate watch, like my Gramp wore in his wesket pocket, and best of all, a beautiful little doll dressed in pink.

I squealed with delight—I had never had a real doll before, only black ones our Mother used to make from old stockings. My Gran found one of her crocheted shawls and I sat by the roaring fire nursing my lovely doll while she got on with the cooking.

Into the oven went the pheasant and potatoes for baking while on the hob a monstrous Christmas pudding bubbled and boiled in the great saucepan. Up to her elbows in flour, my Gran made pastry for mince pies. Her face was red and shiny where she kept bending and peering into the oven as each batch was drawn out.

A COTSWOLD CHRISTMAS

For the hundredth time I peeped at my doll, then I let out a loud scream. 'What ever is the matter my little maid?' my Gran said, rushing over to my side.

'Look Granny, look,' I cried, my cheeks streaming with tears, 'my doll's face, it's gone.'

The heat from the fire had melted the pretty wax face; now all that was left was a shapeless lump. I cried for the rest of the day. I couldn't even eat. I never did taste the pheasant we had prepared so excitedly the day before. As my Gramp ate his Christmas pudding he kept finding shiny threepenny bits. 'Come on my little maid,' he said, 'you might find a florin in your piece.' But it was no use—nothing comforted me.

We went to church the next evening, walking down the beech-lined drive to the village. As we went up the church path a horrid boy snatched my green tammy off by the bobble and I punched him so hard he soon dropped it. 'Proper little spitfire en't you?' he said, but he didn't try it again. My grandparents were slightly ahead of me, chattering, otherwise they would have chastised me for such unseemly behaviour so near to the church.

As the lord and lady of the Manor took their seats in the cold, grey, candle-lit church, the women all curtsied. Her ladyship was dressed in deep purple and sat stiff-backed and regal. Like a proud foreign bird she looked. The brilliant feathers round her

turban-shaped hat wriggled and fluttered at the
slightest movement. She showed up like a jewel
against a sea of the Sunday-best black of the village
folk.

Out in the cold moonlight night once more; good-
nights and ' 'appy New Year if I dun't see 'e agen'
echoed again and again. Then back through the park,
quiet now, save for the hooting owls and scurryings
across the leaf-strewn path of things I couldn't see;

and I held my Gramp's hand tight for fear of being whisked away by witches and hobbly-goblins into the trees.

The next day one of the footmen from the big house knocked at the door of the lodge. He handed a big brown paper parcel to my Gran. 'It's for the little girl,' he said. We stood there for a moment, speechless. 'What ever is it Mr. Carter?' my Gran asked.

'Well Mrs. Broad, her ladyship heard that your little grandchild had had a most unfortunate accident with her doll. There's a note inside,' he said, and was gone.

Still bewildered we went back into the house and I snatched at the wrappings, tearing the paper with excited fingers. 'Careful, child,' my Gran warned, 'it might be something breakable.' She read the note pinned on the top of the box, 'For the pretty little girl in the gay green tammy'. Inside was the biggest, most beautiful doll I had ever seen. My Gran said that it must have belonged to one of her ladyship's children when they were small. It was dressed in fur-trimmed satin and all the clothes took off and I undressed that doll a hundred times or more that day I'm sure. Excitedly I told my Gramp about the doll when he came home from work. He lifted me on his lap and said, 'It's worth all the tea in China to see you laughing again.'

A few days later the baker picked me up. I was

for the pretty
the girl
in the greengrocers tummy.

to travel back home as I had come, and although I'd got my lovely doll and a parcel of things for the rest of the family I cried when I left my grandparents. 'Come again soon little maid,' they said, but I never did.

During the next year my Gran died and my Gramp went to live with my uncle and aunt at a nearby farm. But I spent some very happy holidays with him there.

We used to sit on the wall near the road and he'd sing to me. His favourite was 'Pretty Polly Perkins from Paddington Green'. I've only to hear the tune now and I'm back in that quiet Cotswold village sitting on a wall with my Gramp.

His hair that was once so very black had now turned to what he called 'pepper and salt'—really sprinkled with grey—his eyes brightest blue, crinkled and laughing. And that's how I last saw him, waving goodbye to me as I rode away in the baker's cart that was to take me to Burford. He had given me two super ripe pears to take home but I remember eating them before we got out of the village.

Sometimes I pass the lodge where my grandparents lived for so long and where I spent such happy times. The last occasion was on a cold November day. The place was empty and deserted, the curtainless windows had a ghostly air about them, the Cotswold mist hanging thick in the beech-lined drive, and the last remaining leaves fluttering quietly to the ground. I had a great urge to stop and peer in at the windows. Never go back they say, so I turned away, leaving undisturbed all the lovely memories of the past.

The Little Farm

THE farm where my uncle and aunt lived was set right down in the village of Sherborne, about a mile and a half from the lodge where my Gran and Gramp had lived. And during the school holidays I always went to stay with them for a few weeks.

It was a little farm—I say a 'little' farm because at that time they had only six or eight cows and delivered milk round the village. They had a hand cart they used to push around with a big milk churn in it, and my uncle and cousin would call at the cottages with the milk in steel cans that held about two gallons. Hanging inside the cans were pint and half-pint measures, and at intervals they would refill the cans from the big churn on the hand cart.

The other side-line to this little business of theirs was the lovely buttercup-yellow butter my auntie used to make. First of all she poured the milk from the wide steel pans into a separator, a large mincer-like contraption, hand-turned, and this separated the cream from the milk by some ingenious device so that the cream poured into one pan and the skim milk into another. This skim milk was often fed to the young calves, but poor people with large families would sometimes buy it for about a penny a quart to make milk puddings and other things.

I still seem to hear the monotonous drone that separator made as my auntie tirelessly turned the handle until all the milk that had been set aside had gone through. Then she would pour the thick cream into a wooden butter churn and stand it on the table on its side. Hers had two little wooden legs. Then she would turn the handle which operated the small wooden paddles inside, and before she'd been at it long the wet, sloppy, slap-slap of the paddles changed into a firm and solid sound which meant that the cream had slowly turned into butter.

She'd tip the rough, solid lump of yellow fat out of the churn, then reach for her butter pats. These were flat and made of wood, scrubbed white, and finely ridged, about five inches long and three inches wide, and they had handles. Grasping one in each hand she would pick up one of the yellow lumps, deftly turning it and patting it again and again till it resembled a half-pound slab of butter.

If the weather was very hot my aunt would stack the neat half-pound packs into a large steel bucket, tie a rope to the handle and gradually let the bucket down in the cool well. When the water was about three parts of the way up the outside of the bucket, she'd secure the other end of the rope to a heavy iron bar in the yard—it was always known as the butter bar and I never remember it being used for anything else.

In those days a good deep well was the housewife's only form of keeping food cool, and often meat and milk would be put into buckets and slung down the well until they were needed.

Sometimes if I paid a surprise visit to my aunt's, she would make enough butter specially for my tea. She'd scoop a little thick cream into a jam jar, then, keeping her hand tight over the neck of the jar, she would sit in a chair, shake the jar for about five minutes while we were chatting—then suddenly a lump of yellow would emerge from the cream and she would plop it out on a plate, sprinkle it with a little salt, and cut wafer-thin bread—leaving *me* to spread that wonderfully flavoured rich butter

on, topped with home-made strawberry jam. I don't care what anybody says, and this is not just a fancy of my youth—like perpetual sunshine and things—but that butter my auntie made did taste very different from anything you can buy today.

My Auntie Sarah, like my Gran, was a great wine maker. She was also a good chapel-going body and had a number of friends who were of the same religion. One hot summer I remember she had a couple of lay preachers staying with her for a few days. They were going round to some of the remote villages to preach the gospel and made my auntie's

70

home their temporary headquarters. Both were very much the 'holier than thou' type and firmly believed that any form of 'drink' was a sure passport to hell.

Before they arrived at the farm we carefully moved all the bottles and casks of wine up into a loft over the kitchen. The farm had once been a mill and this loft was where they stored the flour. We had to handle it very gently because some of the wine was still at the fermenting stage, but at least it was out of sight.

As soon as they arrived they started ranting and raging about a young couple who were camping out in a tent near the farm. They had met them as they came down the dusty road—the couple had just come away from the off-licence with bottles of beer under their arms. They did this most days, laying them in the shallow water at the edge of the River Windrush to keep the beer cool and drinkable.

All we heard from the lay preachers was the hell fire and damnation that would surely be the fate of the camping couple and anyone else who took any sort of intoxicating drink. They never stopped. My uncle would catch my eye and look heavenwards as if to say, how much longer have we got to put up with this?

But suddenly their visit was cut short. The afternoon was very hot, threatening thunder, not a breath of air anywhere, and the worthy gentlemen were leading off for the umpteenth time about the sins of the world, and how they were going to convert everybody, when the air was shattered with a loud report, then another and another. Up jumped the black-coated lay preachers, eyes blazing, arms flung heavenwards—'There are the warning notes,' called one in a ranting voice. 'Yes, hell fire and damnation!' shouted the other. 'Judgement on all sinners!'

Just at that moment a red, gory substance started pouring down the walls and onto the white, scrubbed stone floor and settled in a puddle at one of the visitor's feet, and a strong fruity, winey smell filled the room. I took one look at my red-faced aunt and we both went off to get buckets and house flannels to sop up the mess. The visitors stamped out of the house and up the road toward the next village and we never saw them again.

And the only damnation came from my uncle because his favourite wine (raspberry, red- and black-currant) had ended up all over the kitchen floor.

School Days

THE village school, like others of that time, was small and overcrowded. How teachers managed to cram anything into the heads of a bunch of rough country children was a miracle. But with the exception of a few that even a genius could not have taught, we did not turn out too badly—or else where would we be today? Like most of the children, I started school at the tender age of three— five was the proper age, but my mother, like others with large families, was only too glad to get another child off her hands for a few hours.

But those first early days proved to be quite disastrous. It happened that Bern and Bunt, my elder brothers, had taught me a jingle. They seemed to find it very funny and on our way to school kept saying it to me: 'You wants to ask if you can say it to Sir,' Sir being our one-eyed school master, quite kind and very clever.

All that first week we infants played with sand and beads and listened to the frizzy-haired girl who was in charge of us telling stories and nursery rhymes. But I liked the one my brothers had taught me better. And I kept asking 'Miss' if I could tell it to the Headmaster.

The first morning of the second week I was called out front. 'We are all going up to the top class, Mollie. Mr. Westwell wants to hear your poem,' Miss said. We traipsed up; I walked boldly, swaggeringly, showing off. I was to say my piece in front of the whole school! The Headmaster lifted me up and stood me on his desk. 'Silence!' he said. 'Let the youngest pupil in the school recite.'

Beaming boldly I began,

A KIND OF MAGIC

Nipple, Nipple with one eye—

From the back of the room I could see my brothers, taller than the rest of the kids. Bunt had gone very red and Bern was waving to me. I waved back and went on,

> *Went to Church on Sundays,*
> *Prayed to God to give him strength*
> *To whack the kids on Mondays.*

There was a deadly hush and then suddenly the air was rent with the loud whacking of Mr. Westwell's cane as it came down on the desk, and I nearly fell off with fright. I noticed he had turned the colour of my mother's geraniums. Something was wrong—no clapping from the class, just silence. Suddenly I was seized, turned over and tanned on the backside several times. Bawling and screaming I ran out of the room, round by the pond and the church and home. And my first public appearance was ended.

Because of this incident our mother took us away from the village school and we all trailed up to Witney for a little while, but I remember nothing of this short period. Then the old school master at Ducklington retired and we returned to the village school.

By then, fortunately for us, a Mr. and Mrs. Preston had been appointed. He was Headmaster, teaching standards 4, 5, 6, and 7, and his wife taught the lower classes. They were a marvellous pair, kind and understanding and just what we needed in the village. They were fresh and young and loved by all.

After school some of us would stay behind and practice for the concerts that they tirelessly arranged. Dressed in clothes that Mrs. Preston contrived, we became Kings and Queens, Princes and Pages. To a bunch of uncouth village children this was wonderful. Our stage in the parish room where the concerts were performed consisted of a number of trestle tables, erected carefully to make them safe to walk on. Everybody turned out to these events to see 'ower little 'uns' perform. We did not realize that these brief concerts were helping us to grow up—to talk properly and make it possible to converse with people.

To our school came children from outlying villages and hamlets. They often had to cross a couple of muddy fields before walking the two or three miles to Ducklington. One of these small places was called Yelford, just a manor house, a farm, four cottages and a church in a field. One very big family who lived at Yelford used to pick up eight or ten loaves of bread after school, carrying it home in hessian sacks slung across their backs. To keep the bread moist their mother used to stack it in the church font. Their cottage was very near to the little church and it was easy to slip out and get a loaf. The big family left little storage room in the cottage for such a lot of bread.

Another family who lived in one of the hamlets took on the delivery of the newspapers, both in our village and where they lived. They walked from their home for three miles to collect the daily papers and delivered to most of the cottages in our village before school. Then during the dinner-time they delivered the rest. But the people who lived in their own hamlet had to wait until after school for theirs.

At school, boys and girls played together in a small playground where there were four bucket lavatories for the girls and four for the boys, separated by sheets of corrugated iron. The boys used to try and frighten the girls in all sorts of ways, and once one of them put a great hedgehog in a newly emptied bucket. Then they waited for the first girl to go in.

It happened to be a timid, rather shy girl and fairly new to the school. She saw the animal just as she was about to sit down and, letting out a loud scream, came rushing out with her long, white, lace-edged drawers hanging round her knees. Then they fell to her ankles and she went headlong, full length onto the hard playground. The screaming and shouting brought out Mr. Preston and all the boys got six of the best.

In the playground kids fought and played and called each other names—

> *'Oodley, 'oodley,*
> *Stick stack stoodley,*
> *Eyeball, beball,*
> *Long-legged 'oodley.*

79

someone would chant to us Woodleys, although the same rhyme could be used for other names. For the short-legged Fishers, for instance:

> *Fisher, Fisher,*
> *Stick stack stisher,*
> *Eyeball, beball,*
> *Short-legged Fisher.*

A favourite way of answering back was:

> *Sticks and stones*
> *May break my bones*
> *But names will never hurt me.*

Children who told tales had this bawled to them in the street:

> *Tell-tale tit,*
> *Cut your throat a slit,*
> *All the sense that you've got*
> *Is in your mother's teapot.*

When there was a General Election children proudly wore a coloured ribbon according to their parents' politics—although grown-ups would never admit which party they fancied. We Conservatives would link arms and chant:

Vote, vote, vote for Major Edmondson.
Who's that knocking at the door?
If it's Bennett or it's Fry [Liberal and Labour
    candidates]

SCHOOL DAYS

We'll sock 'um in the eye
And never see their faces any more.

And we'd snatch ribbons off other children if they happened to be wearing anything other than blue.

At school you could catch head-lice quicker than measles and our mother dreaded the time when we

might be sent home by 'The Bug Nurse' or 'Nitty Norah', as some of us called the health nurse who came to our school about once a month to examine everybody's head. As soon as she walked in our teacher would say 'Heads down, children,' and we all folded our arms across the desks and rested our heads on them. Before this public examination the teacher would have a whispered conversation with the nurse, probably about those children who were known always to be cooty. These were sent out to wait in the porch, where we hung our coats, then they were sent home and told not to come back until their mothers had got their heads clean.

During the very cold weather we used to take our dinner to school. Our mother would pack up great hunks of bread and dripping or lumps of cold bread pudding and give us each a screw of paper that contained a spoonful of sugar and cocoa. Our teacher would put a kettle of water on the tortoise stove so that we might make a hot drink—that is, if we hadn't eaten the dry mixture beforehand.

After a couple of years Mr. Preston fell ill and they left, and a Miss Spencer became Headmistress. The lower classes were taught by shy, kindly, plump Miss Evans. She was young and pretty and I worshipped her. She did her hair up in a knot at the back and wore crocheted jumpers that I could see through and she had dimples in her arms just above the elbows. Her voice was quiet but firm and when she read poetry to us it used to make me cry.

One Christmas she gave me a present of a lovely handkerchief. Stamped on it was a figure of a Spanish lady, dressed in red. It was the first handkerchief I had ever possessed—bits of old sheeting were doled out to our family for nose-blowing, and always pinned on the jersey or frock of the younger members so as not to lose them. I could do nothing wrong while I was in Miss Evans's class. 'Teacher's pet' they called me while I was there for I was always top, except for sums.

Too soon it was time to move up to Miss Spencer's. She came from somewhere in Lincolnshire and pronounced her words in a different way from us in our small Oxfordshire village. We would be in the middle of a singing lesson—suddenly she would stop playing the piano, jump up, stamp her foot and say—'It's moon, moon, moon, not moo-oon as you say it.' Words like 'round' and 'bound' and lots of others she tried to make us say differently. But it was useless for her to try to alter a dialect that our mothers and fathers and the whole family spoke. One prim little miss couldn't alter centuries of speech. Whereas Miss Evans brought out the best in us, Miss Spencer seemed to do just the opposite —at least for me.

I don't think she was used to country children anyhow. She was small and pinched-looking and had soft white hands, and catching hold of them in country dancing was like holding a sponge. She wasn't used to our rough ways and would squirm when kids brought in frogs and frog spawn, and fat-backed toads. One boy, Doungey Clarke, brought a couple of harmless grass snakes into school, hidden in his cap, and she squealed the place down. We had no respect for her at all.

Older boys of thirteen and fourteen were some-times head and shoulders taller than Miss Spencer. When she called them out to cane them for some trifling offence they just snatched the cane from her. And once Chris Goodwin, a great lump of a lad, picked her up and dumped her down on the tortoise stove—thankfully it was summertime. How we giggled and sniggered to see her skinny legs dang-ling in space!

Then suddenly one Monday morning she was not there. She had gone back to Lincolnshire in a hurry. Stories flashed round the village like wildfire—she was supposed to have been secretly in love with a confirmed bachelor. The poor fellow would have nothing to do with her and, filled with frustration, she packed her bags and left.

That summer our school lessons were continued by a Miss Seed who came pedalling over the Aston Hills to fill in for our departed Miss Spencer. She arrived on an old upright bicycle—'Seedie's bedstead' we called it. But she was jolly and understanding, and above all fair. In the past there had been too much discrimination between the very poor kids and the better-off ones.

It was while she was in charge of us that I won 'The Bishop's prize' for scripture. As my hand shot up to answer the examiner's questions I could see her encouraging smile time and time again almost saying, that's it, my girl, you can do it. I still have the prize, the only thing I have ever won. Inside the worn, red-covered Prayer Book is written: 'Presented to Mollie Woodley, Ducklington School, after an examination held on the 17th of June 1927. Signed: William Preedy, Assistant Diocesan Inspector.

As it was a church school we often attended services during weekdays—Ascension Day, Saints' days and Empire Day, and once a year we all solemnly took an egg to a church service, carefully laying our small offering in a yellow wicker washing basket that was placed near the altar. The eggs were afterwards packed up and taken to Oxford on the train, and then on to the Radcliffe Infirmary.

On Empire day we all got up early to go into the meadows to pick daisies, which we made into daisy chains to drape on our dresses and garlands for our heads and waists, wrists and ankles. Then after a short church service we would all troop out to the small green by the school and march round saluting the Union Jack.

On the 29th May, bedecked with sprigs of oak apple, we linked arms on our way to school and chanted—

> *Shick Shack day,*
> *Twenty-ninth of May,*
> *If we don't have a holiday*
> *We'll all run away.*

And woe betide any kid not wearing a sprig of oak. Gangs of us set on such offenders, stinging them all over with nettles.

There were no facilities for anything other than just ordinary lessons at our small school. It was a three-roomed building with part of one room screened off for the infants. When we reached the age of thirteen we girls walked up to Witney once a week to attend cookery and housewifery lessons and the boys went on a different day to learn woodwork. We girls were taught how to make cornflour moulds and rice puddings, and how to turn out rooms and do laundering, while the boys made stools and tea trays, and we all learned a new way of life in town.

Some of the town kids looked upon us as a bunch of hobbledehoys; they called us names and teased us about our rough clothes. 'You be one a they dungle-bred 'Oodleys from Duckleton' a pale-faced, runny-nosed girl said to me one day, and I set about her and we fought like a couple of cats—nobody called me 'dungle-bred' after that.

Sitting in school on hot summer days we could hear the cows going by, to and from milking, with Mr. Druce calling them, 'cup, cup, cup', and occasionally shouting to Blossom or Jenny for stopping to pull grass from the churchyard. The village pond was just outside the classroom and we could hear the cows splash into the green slimy water where they would stand like statues, cooling their great hot bodies; then we would hear the slosh-slosh as their long pink tongues picked up the water.

There were always ducks on the pond, just a few. They belonged to Mrs. Lija Collis who lived near by. Any time of the day her precious birds could be seen waddling across the green that separated her cottage from the pond, or swimming or standing on their heads searching for food on the slimy bottom. A reward if we ever found a duck's egg was a super piece of home-made cake—how we searched and prayed to find an egg in the rushes or in the rough grass near the water!

A KIND OF MAGIC

Recently I came across these few lines in a book—

> *Four ducks on a pond,*
> *A grass-bank beyond,*
> *A blue sky of spring,*
> *White clouds on the wing:*
> *What a little thing*
> *To remember for years—*
> *To remember with tears!*

They were written by William Allingham and someone had scribbled on the top in pencil, 'Ducklington Pond'.

Not that there was always a blue sky of spring; in winter the pond was often frozen solid for weeks on end and we would spend many happy hours sliding there. In summer we made mud pies on its fly-filled sides and most all of us at some time fell in, but our parents were probably none the wiser because, as we played all through the long hot summer days, our clothes just dried on us.

Some of the carters were very kind and would give us a ride up the village or from Witney if we had been on an errand. I loved to ride on Holtoms' flour carts. Carter Porter used to sit up front, covered in a fine white dust of flour; even his eyelashes were powdered with the stuff. Sometimes he would have three, other times four, great cart horses in the shafts depending on the weight of the load. The great sacks of flour were stacked in the long Oxfordshire wagon and in the summertime the horses wore little white caps with blue and red bobbles on over their ears to keep the flies from worrying them, and their tails would be tied up with red and blue too. And always the horses wore harness brasses that winked and shone in the sunshine.

When Carter Porter drove the team to Witney he would start tapping the horses just before he got to the station hill so that they could pull the great load up better. When we got to the top he would stop and jump down and slip under one of the back wheels a thing he called a shoe brake. It was flat and about a foot long and it stopped the wheel from turning, and this helped to steady the loaded wagon downhill.

At the goods station he would skilfully back the horses and cart right up the track where he and the railway workers unloaded the flour into a railway wagon. But not before he had hung great brown nosebags filled with chaff round the horses' necks, and they would stand and munch contentedly, occasionally blowing into their food. When the bag was nearly empty they would toss it up, flinging their heads high, to enable them to get all the bits at the bottom of the nosebag.

When it was raining, carters and farm workers used to sit hunched up on their carts with sacks tied over their heads and shoulders. Some of them disliked us kids hanging on the backs of the carts and they would give a backward flick with their whips, narrowly missing, just to let us know that we were not to hang on, let alone ride. But when you had walked backwards and forwards to school twice and then had to run an errand up to the town, a little help, even from a muck cart, was welcome.

At harvest time we used to go out into the fields where the men were busy loading the sheaves and cadge a ride on the leading horse. Up and down all day from the farm to the fields I've ridden on the fat brown rump of old Turpin; so big he was he filled the shafts of the yellow farm wagon.

Then one day on our way home from school we came across a little knot of people, so we joined them, pushing forward to see what had happened. Turpin lay helpless in the roadway, his huge brown eyes rolling, his once active body now still and useless. 'Dun 'is bit, no good to nobody now,' one of the old men said. Someone sent for the knacker man, and crying bitterly we watched them drag the heavy animal, now dead, onto the floor of the cart. Then, roped and chained, he was taken away.

The incident worried me for days, until our mother took me quietly on her lap and explained that Turpin's soul had gone where the fields were always filled with sweet grass and scented clover. There would be no more hard work—no more clouts on his brown rump for not going fast enough —nothing to do all day but roam about in those evergreen glades with other animals. And the picture of a heaven filled with cropping horses put my mind at rest.

A little while afterwards Clarke's horse fell down and died, and I didn't feel too bad at all.

A KIND OF MAGIC

One day I was sent up to Witney to get two twopenny oranges for Bunt who was in bed with tonsillitis.

When it was fine we never went the road way to the town but took a short cut through 'The Moors', across a footpath that lay over three or four fields with tiny wooden bridges spanning the green-slimed ditches.

I was dawdling back home, lazily dangling a plimsolled foot into the almost stagnant water. It was scorching hot. Fat cows grazed in the fields, tails swinging like pendulums. Clouds of flies hung over the manure-covered paths. I grabbed a handful of azzies (the local name for haws) and chewed away as contentedly as the cows.

Suddenly from behind the hedge came one of the village lads—he was a great gangling boy of about fourteen and a bit on the simple side.

'Hello,' he said. 'I got summut fer you,' and he came towards me, cap in hand. In the cap were about a dozen bright-red crab-apples.

He handed them to me with one hand and grabbed hold of me with the other. 'I got summut else fer you too,' he whispered hoarsely, with a wild animal look on his face. 'You come down yer with I,' and he half-dragged me towards the hedge.

I struggled, wrenching myself free, tossing the cap full of crab-apples in his red sweaty face and rushed stumbling over the grass. I lost my oranges as I ran over the fields, blindingly crying, breathless and terror-stricken. I reached the stile and roadway before I dare look round to see if he was following.

Just then one of the carters from the flour mill came riding by on his wagon. He pulled up the horses to a stop.

'Come on young Mollie, what's up wi' you? En't never sin you cryin' affor'.'

He sat me up beside him. I tried to answer him but no sound came out. 'I've lost me oranges,' I blurted out at last. 'They're for our Bunt. 'E en't very well.'

'Never mind, one of the others 'ull go an' find 'um,' he said, as he set me down outside our gate.

Our mother was in the garden. 'She's lost her oranges, poor little mite. Proper upset 'er is too,' he called out.

'I'll give her "lost her oranges",' she cried. 'That was my last few coppers till Saturday,' and she boxed my ears as I ran indoors. 'Go on off to bed with you. That'll teach you not to waste good money,' she called after me as I crept upstairs.

Betty was sent back over 'The Moors'. She found the oranges all right. 'There was crab-apples scattered all over the place,' she told our Mother. 'Bin wastin' 'er time picking them sour things I reckon.'

Hop, Skip and Jump

THERE was no special time to start certain games.
For weeks we all might be skipping madly, then one
day someone would come to school with a bag of
marbles or a whip and top, and suddenly all the
other children did the same. For when errands had
been run or our small daily tasks had been completed we would spend the long summer evenings
playing contentedly, all the while trying to play our
chosen game as well as or better than our brothers
and sisters, or the kids next door.

Probably many of the games had been handed
down from earlier generations—ring games and
ball games with singing and rhymes to accompany
them, although some of the words most likely had
lost their original meaning.

Some of the games needed more than one child to
play them, but it was nothing to see a small solitary

figure, pig-tailed and pinafored, bouncing a ball against a wall while counting, reciting, chanting or singing. The idea was to keep the ball in play through an ever-changing, intricate sequence of movements. The first dozen times it was simply thrown against the wall and caught, then bounced under the right leg, then under the left leg and finally bounced onto the wall again while the player spun round and caught it in mid-air.

Another ball game was Alary:

> One, two, three, alary
> My ball went down the cary
> Serves you right for playing alary
> On a Sunday morning.

The first time each word of the rhyme was spoken the ball was bounced, but on repeating it the pattern was changed. We would bounce the ball, throw the right leg over, and when we could bounce it with the left hand and throw the left leg over, then our cup was full. To perfect these games was our aim and it did not matter how long it took.

Skipping was often done by solitary children. Our mother disliked the skipping craze because we wore out so much boot leather, but skip we would. Some of the children possessed proper ropes with nicely shaped wooden handles all painted red and blue. Poorer children had to be contented with any old bit of thick string they could get hold of. Skipping

HOP, SKIP AND JUMP

games usually started with a slowly spoken jingle. 'Salt, mustard, vinegar, pepper,' we would chant, then speed up the rope to finish with an exultant 'one hundred'.

Other Oxfordshire rhymes were—

> *Black-currant, red-currant,*
> *Raspberry jam,*
> *Tell me the name*
> *Of your young man*

or

> *Cups and saucers,*
> *Plates and dishes,*
> *Here comes a man*
> *In calico breeches.*

97

As we progressed we could skip backwards—at least the rope was twirled backwards, or with the arms across the chest. And if you could jump in the air while the rope was twirled twice under your feet then you were really happy.

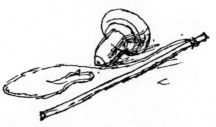

Whips and tops were most popular in the spring when the roads began to dry and clean from mud and muck. You could buy a top for a ha'penny. There were different sorts, and we had a special name for each: Carrot, Granny, Window Breaker or Spinny Jinny. They were usually made of plain white wood but we would crayon the tops so that when they spun round they looked quite pretty.

The shortage of string for the whips presented problems, and who could afford to buy string? If we could get one of the older boys or girls who worked in the blanket mills at Witney to bring us a bit of 'mill bonding', a thickish, strong white string —only used in the mills—then we were well-away.

There was an art in keeping a top going by just thrashing it with a whip. The trouble with the 'window breakers'—sleek, slim tops they were—

was the fact that they flew in the air as you whacked them, and if your aim was bad they often smashed straight through somebody's front window. Then there was hell to pay—at least the offender's parents were expected to buy new window glass. In the meanwhile the precious top and whip were flung on the back of the fire.

Hoops was another game that was hard on boot leather. Some of the boys had large iron hoops which they steered skilfully with an iron hook; for miles and miles they bowled them. Girls, if they were lucky, had smaller wooden ones which they tapped gently with a stick—mostly we used old bicycle wheels or tyres and got just as much fun out of them.

Of course, marbles was a summer craze, a slower, quieter game, and if you had a penny you could buy twenty chalk marbles. A Tally, which was the one you scattered the smaller ones with, usually cost a farthing and was often made of clear glass with bright, multi-coloured wavy threads in. If you were lucky enough to find an empty lemonade bottle that had been thrown away, a sharp crack on a stone broke the bottle and released a super glass Tally for nothing. Boys *and* girls played the game, but it was really considered more of a boy's game. The marbles were carried around in flannel bags secured tightly at the top with a thread of tape.

Once, from somewhere, I'd got four marbles and a glass tally and one night after school I plagued the champion of the village to play. He was a big bully of a lad and sniggered as I challenged him. 'I shall take your few fust game, you see if I dun't! Hark at 'er challenging I, thur yent nobody in the school as can beat I.'

It was true too, and he and his followers used to walk to the other villages and challenge the kids there. 'Set 'um up then Mollie, we en't got long to 'ang about yer, we be awf up to Witney tu beat some a they tonight.' We placed our marbles on the dusty road against the school wall. 'You go fust,' Bert said, 'cost if you dun't you wun't 'ave no chance at all tu play.'

I took careful aim and scattered the row of chalk marbles. 'Coo!' one of the other boys said, 'that was a lucky aim.' I quickly picked up my winnings.

'Beginner's luck—thas what that was,' Bert sniggered. He stood well back, took aim at the fresh row we had set up—and missed!

'Crikey! Wass up wi you?' Percy Russell said. 'Strikes I you be nervous Bert.'

For the next half hour we played and Bert the Bully never won a game. The other boys were shouting and cheering me on and Bert was swearing and getting redder and redder. Then it came to the pitch when he set his last few marbles in a row. Spitting on his hands he swore he'd beat me yet. But he didn't, and mad with temper he flung his super lucky tally at me, hitting me sharply in the face.

'There, take that!' he said. 'I'll win 'um all back tomorrow, you see if I dun't.' Then he and his gang moved off, shouting and swearing. I stuffed my winnings into Bert's flannel marble bag that he'd left lying on the ground and ran off home.

When I got to school next morning Bert and his gang were bowling their iron hoops in the playground. 'En't you going tu try and win 'um back?' I asked, clutching my bag of marbles.

'No I blumen well en't,' he said. 'Shove off. Marbles is a girl's game,' and they tore away and charged round the playground like a herd of young bullocks. In fact nobody wanted to play. They were all too busy bowling their hoops.

During the dry weather we girls played hopscotch—we would mark out the 'beds' with a bit of rough stone, which acted as chalk if you found a good white piece. Sometimes the 'bed' would be six large squares joined together and in each square a number was written. The art of the game was to slide a small, flattish stone from one square to the next. This was done by hopping on one foot and gently kicking the stone along with the other so that it landed right on the number. If the stone slid too far or landed on a line then the player had to start again. The winner was the one who could complete the game without any faults.

Another hopscotch 'bed' was marked out like a giant snailshell. This was a much more complicated

way of playing, and all sorts of instructions were
written in the different squares. You had to con-
centrate like mad to be able to master this game—
still on one leg. You could play this on your own,
but it was much more exciting if two or more took
part.

A KIND OF MAGIC

There was little or no traffic on the roads and so, as we walked to school, many of us played games on the way. Six or seven of us would link arms—right across the narrow road we would stretch, singing:

> *Queen, Queen Caroline,*
> *Dipped her hair in the turpentine.*
> *The turpentine made it shine,*
> *Queen, Queen Caroline.*

(I planned to try this when I grew up.)
Or

> *Here we go gathering nuts and may*
> *on a cold and frosty morning,*

fitting other words to this tune as we rushed along:

> *This is the way we run to school*

or

> *Jump in the air and clap our hands,*

and before we knew where we were we'd walked the mile and a half, and were boiling into the bargain.

The most popular game for boys was 'Fox and Hounds'. On clear frosty winter nights they would run for miles and miles. The lad chosen for the fox had to be a pretty good runner. He would dash off into the night and a little later the hounds would follow, shouting as they ran, 'Come out wherever you are, the dogs are on your tracks.'

Sometimes the fox would 'holler' and give his pursuers an idea as to where he was. Then the hounds would be off in full cry, but the 'fox' often doubled back and they would be lucky to find him. Often, after hours of chasing and running, the 'dogs' failed to catch their man and the game would be continued the next night until the fox was caught; then another was chosen to take his place.

Then a change came over our lives. About the middle of the 'twenties a travelling concert party settled on the outskirts of the town near by.

They had a huge tent with wooden forms stacked in tiers. There were thre'penny and sixpenny seats down front. The ha'penny seats, very high, were just rows of boards set almost underneath the tent top. 'Going to the ha'penny leg dangle?' we'd say. And halfway through the 'Death of Little Willy' like as not you were all suffering from acute pins and needles. But they were exciting nights.

We saw 'Maria Martin in the Red Barn' or the 'Death of Little Eva', 'Uncle Tom's Cabin', and many others.

It was a family affair, this concert party. Mother, father and sons and daughters-in-law. I had a silent crush on one of the lads performing. He looked so handsome as I worshipped him from the ha'pennies.

Then I saw him close-up one day with all his make-up on. He looked like a Red Indian and was ever so old—quite thirty! That cured me.

Of course there was a picture house in the town but the cheapest seats were three-ha'pence for Saturday afternoon matinée. Most of the children went then.

When I got a bit older (I think I was about thirteen at the time), I was asked to deliver to every house in the village a pamphlet on which was printed a month's programme of what was on at 'The People's Palace'. For doing this I was given a free pass once a week.

They were all silent films, of course, with Mr. Lewis playing the piano down front. Many of the children could not read and bigger brothers or sisters read the captions out loud—when half the audience was reading out loud there was a tidy din going on all the time.

But it wasn't all games—there were errands to be run, often up to the town after school, or kindling wood to be gathered from the nearest hedge. And younger brothers and sisters always needed to be taken for walks while our mother was cooking the evening meal. 'Take them down the Curbridge Road,' Mother would call as we started off. The Curbridge road was very quiet, just a country lane really.

As we walked between the thick, berried hedgerows we gorged ourselves with wild berries, fruits and leaves, suffering no more than severe stomach-ache. 'Bread and cheese', the new leaves of the May bush, were eaten as fast as they grew. Even to this day, when the warm spring sun opens those tender green leaves, I still greedily gather some, savouring those halcyon days.

Somehow we all knew what not to eat when it came to poisonous berries and things. I suppose it was something that was automatically handed down from one generation to another for I never ever remembered anyone being poisoned. But we did have a pet jackdaw who, attracted by some poisonous berries that we had picked to decorate the home with, decided to sample them. We found him dead on the sideboard. Everybody cried and we buried him in the garden, and for a few days placed flowers on the tiny mound.

We knew where the first dewy mushrooms grew,

and the fattest blackberries, and called every field around by its special name—not the official one, but by association with something or other:—'The Devil's nutting ground', 'Stranges' lucerne', the 'flower field', 'Parker's forty acres', 'Clark's moon daisy ground'.

There were green lanes between some of the fields and these provided short cuts to the next hamlet or village. And double hedges where we would find our 'first of the year' primroses and violets or where we'd play for hours in bramble caves.

We would climb trees and make swings by half–bending, half-breaking willow branches. Then catching firmly hold of the branch and with our feet pressed against the trunk of the tree, we would push off, letting the branch swing us high into the air before dropping down again. It was a tremendous thrill—but we had to be quick on the down-drop for if our feet missed the trunk we were bashed against it. Up and down, up and down we would swing, for hours on end.

There was great competition in our house as to who found the first flowers as they started to bloom. We had no other reward than a good warm hug from our mother and a little praise because we had been more observant than the others. But this made us sharp-sighted and keen, always on the look out, a gentle way of instilling in our minds knowledge that we were to find useful for the rest of our lives.

Lotions and Potions

OUR childhood illnesses were either cured or treated by our mothers; having a Doctor was almost unheard of unless someone elderly was dying of a painful and incùrable disease, for it cost money. So home cures were widely used, some of them quite primitive too. Our mother had some magical cures handed down to her from her mother—hot, spicy and almost medieval they were; a pinch of this and a sprinkling of that, and taken so hot they nearly seared your throat.

I can see her now, bending over us, in one hand a tablespoonful of one of her special concoctions, and in the other a spoonful of jam—the offending medicine was pushed into our unwilling mouths, our eyes shut tight so as not to see. Then immediately afterwards, the jam was thrust down our throats in an effort to camouflage the horrible taste. Mind you, if you could keep the concoction down, the cure for whatever you had was certain.

Our winter salvation, apart from the great suet puddings we ate, was surely our 'possibles', a name we christened the flannel weskit we younger ones were annually sewn up in. At the beginning of the cold weather our Mother slapped goose-grease thickly on our backs and chests, then sewed us up in a piece of real flannel—next to the skin. This was kept on till spring! No proper baths were taken during the winter; we were merely topped and tailed—washed up as far as possible and down as far as possible, 'possible' being that smelly greasy flannel weskit that was in such a state at the end of the winter that it was simply cut off our bodies and flung in the fire.

When we were small the only thing we were ever given to cure a bad head cold was a steaming hot basin of bread and milk. But when we got older home-made wine was the answer, heated with a red-hot poker and drunk at once. We would stagger upstairs after a hot toddy of elderberry wine and fling ourselves sweating into bed—and get up the next morning as fit as a fiddle. Other people swore by black-currant tea for colds and coughs. This was just a good spoonful of home-made black-currant jam in a cup of boiling water.

Some of the villagers had originated from different parts of the country, bringing with them their own special potions and lotions and beliefs. Our next-door neighbour's daughter was supposed to be 'weak in the chest' and she was never seen without her 'velvety band' as her mother called it. It was a narrow, black velvet band fastened tightly round her neck, and this was only taken off when she washed. She wore this well into her teens and for all I know she may be still wearing one.

Some of the older men and women carried either a potato or a nutmeg about with them believing that this warded off 'The Rheumatics', the symptoms being any ache or pain they had anywhere in their body.

Others walked around with a number of little leather bags hung round their waists next to the skin; this was really a secret way of believing, and what was in the bags was anybody's guess. Once our mother, very unwillingly, was forced to help lay an old man out ('get him ready to meet his Maker' was the expression often used). And he had a number of these little leather bags tied round his waist; how long they had been there remained a mystery. They opened some of the bags and whatever had been in them had completely disappeared.

There was never any need to put up with warts for long. One old lady could charm them away simply by rubbing them either with the inside of a broad-bean pod or with one of those huge black slugs, the latter being used when broad beans were not in season. Always in the winter we would rub our chilblained feet with raw onions to try and ease the itching, and a small piece of real silk was carefully hoarded away by most families to be used if anyone had a stye on the eye: first the silk had to be drawn through a gold wedding ring and then the stye was stroked with the silk twelve times night and morning. A general relief for earache and toothache was a small flannel bag filled with common salt. The salt-filled bag would be put in the oven to get it well and truly hot and this would be held against the pain.

My elder sister used to get up very early on

summer mornings and go out to Pudney's field and bathe her face in the morning dew in an effort to get rid of her crop of freckles. Some cottagers swore by nettle beer for clearing the blood, others made a concoction with pearl barley, liquorice, figs and raisins. And one old lady used to make butter-cup ointment by boiling flowers and vaseline to-gether, and her almost wrinkle-free face was a proof of its worth.

One of my Gran's special herb salves was made simply with home-cured lard and freshly gathered groundsel, elderflower and wormwood all boiled up together. This was kept and used for any sores or to bring a bruise out, and if my Gramp had a lame sheep he would rub the animal's foot or leg with the same stuff.

A KIND OF MAGIC

Our mother was a great believer in bread poultices to bring a boil to a head or to slap red-hot on to any gathering or festered place, but a farm labourer who lived near by swore by hot cow dung.

Friday night was 'jollop night' in our house whether you needed it or not: either the juice from soaked senna pods or brimstone and treacle was the order of the day. Later on we had Beecham's Pills and I remember reading on the wooden lid the words 'worth a guinea a box', and wondered how on earth our mother could afford these.

Village Life

IN spring, when it was warm enough, we all took a weekly bath in the old wash-house where coal and wood was kept and the washing done. The copper would be well stoked up with hedge wood and filled up with water from the well. Then we would take it in turns to sit in our mother's zinc washing bath, just adding a drop more hot water as each of us stepped in.

In summer there was no need for baths; dozens of us would go down to the River Windrush, bathing and teaching ourselves to swim. Every now and then we would take a bit of soap and have a good wash in the river and this saved our mother the job of filling up the old copper.

Older men who didn't go swimming had what was called 'a swabble down' during hot weather. I've seen my stepfather stripped to the waist, sloshing water over his arms and shoulders. This was always done outside in the garden and the soapy water left in the bowl was usually tipped over plants—nothing was wasted, not even soapy water.

VILLAGE LIFE

One of the villagers, Mrs. Pye, used to make a song and dance about their washing habits. She'd say to our mother on a warm day: 'Ah, Missus, I be goin' tu light a fire in the hovel [wash-house] an' when that water's good an' hot I be goin' tu wash my fit an' legs an' ower gel, 'er's a goin' tu wash 'er fit an' legs, and then George [her husband] he's goin' tu rurely wash 'is fit an' legs'—so we always thought of George as a person with much dirtier feet and legs than his wife or daughter.

They came from a remote village north of the county and pronounced their words differently from most of us, and had the most peculiar expressions too. Mrs. Pye was as thin as a whip stick. She would pull her skirt out at the waist and say 'Lar' Missus, I be slipping 'ud'—like a woodnut slips its hud she meant, and when she was hungry she'd say, 'My back varnear touches my belly I be that lear, proper famaled I be.' When she did her housework she always wore a coarse 'epern'—an apron made from a clean washed sack—and a man's cap perched on top of her bun of hair. A great long hatpin kept the cap firmly in place, and her skirts were long and black.

When her daughter was engaged Mrs. Pye came along to our house and asked our mother to come and have a look at the present that the young man had given her daughter. ' 'Tis lovely Missus, a sort of pos-set thing, creamy white with roses on.' At that time young girls were using a thing called a 'poshet'. This was a small flat handbag, often made of raffia, and this was what our mother thought she was going to see. Imagine her surprise when she walked into Mrs. Pye's cottage to see, set out on the white scrubbed kitchen table, a full set of bedroom ware, jug, basin, chamber pots and all, creamy white with roses on.

A year or so after this Mrs. Pye's daughter and the young man decided that they would be married. So about three weeks before the great day Mrs. Pye, eager to show the fellow what a good steady thrifty girl he'd got, suggested that he should be invited to see what the girl had saved up in her bottom drawer. It was rather cold weather just then, so she said to our mother, 'Ah, I be going tu light a fire in the bedroom and ower gel's going tu show 'er young man all 'er got.'

There was a woman who always seemed to be having babies and she had a rather nice way of telling folks that she was pregnant. She would hug her stomach and say, 'Well bein' as I be as I be'. And sometimes the menfolk could be heard to say, without any hint of vulgarity, when their wives were having another child, 'Damn me if 'er en't bin an' joined the puddin' club agen'. And illegitimate children were referred to as 'Sun-hatched' or 'Love children'.

Since a visit from the Doctor was so rare, if anyone had to call him in they would remember for years what he had said. This would be repeated and savoured to relatives and friends, although the teller sometimes got the words a bit mixed—'The Doctor says thur's nothin' 'e can do for I, its summat *eternal*, but 'e wouldn't say no more'—a story one woman was very fond of telling.

And a new young Doctor at his first practice called on one old lady and enquired how she was: 'Middlin',' the woman replied, and the Doctor used to tell the tale against himself of how he went

straight back and searched the medical journal to try and find out what 'middlin' ' meant.

Villagers just didn't greet each other with a simple 'Good morning' but would probably follow it up with 'how bistthis morning then, George?' 'Ah,' the other would reply, 'I be rough an' ready like a rat catcher's dog'; or seeing his pal looking a bit glum, he might say, 'I be in the pink, but you looks as if you worked hard for a bob an' found 'twas a bad un'. Or, 'you looks as crusty as a barrow-load of muck on a frosty morning'.

When people spoke of walking anywhere they often used to say that they were going by 'Walker's bus'. Ask how they were and the answer would most likely be, 'Ah! Bad abed an' wus up' or 'None the better for your askin' '.

Typical Oxfordshire expressions were heard every day: 'bissent' was used instead of 'you are not', and 'cyassent' instead of 'cannot'.

They called left-handed folk 'keky-handed', thin folk 'herrin'-gutted' and loud--mouthed men and women 'chopsey'. A person who talked a lot was called a 'chattermag' and an awkward one was 'tiziky' or 'cussed'. Anyone slow-witted or stupid was 'dummul-headed'.

If Mr. Pye, who lived near us, was talking about going to the parish tea and our mother might ask politely, 'Well, who else is going?', instead of saying everybody in the village he'd say 'Well, thee and I and all of us'.

Young men spoke of 'wenchin' ' when they went out after the girls, and when people roamed about the fields it was called 'pelvering' or 'traipsin' '—

never walking. 'Ketch holt', they'd say, if they wanted anybody to catch hold of anything, and if you sat thinking you'd be 'mumchancing'. 'What's 'e gawpin' at?', villagers would remark if a stranger was staring at them.

The times, when I was small, I've asked grownups where they were going, only to be put off by them answering 'Round the park to see the shops' or 'Thur and back to see how far 'tis'!

The sky over to the west was always known as 'Round Will's Mother's way'. The expression came from a girl who had married a fellow called Will from Brize Norton, a village that lay west of Ducklington. And if the clouds were black and lowery in that direction she'd say, 'That looks black round Will's Mother's way', and to this day all our family, wherever they are, still use the expression.

The word 'unkid' was used instead of horrible or nasty, and 'flummoxed' instead of worried or bothered. 'He do ugger mugger I so', the old lady next to us used to say of her husband who was one of the world's worst worriers.

Men who came home from the fields with muddy boots came home 'all clapered up'.

If a child came home with his clothes ragged they would be 'torn to lickutts' instead of to pieces.

Children were called 'childern' and stones 'Stwons', and the word 'dillin' was the name for the smallest pig in a litter, but was also used to describe a child who was small and undernourished.

Grown-ups referred to a tall thin child as gawky, but we kids would sing out after one as he went by, 'You be long and lanky, thin and cranky'.

Superstitions, bad and good luck omens, ran riot in the village, especially with the older folk, although we children believed in them too. There were, and still are, women who never dreamt of washing blankets during the month of May.

> *Wash blankets in May,*
> *You'll soon be under clay.*

There were old ladies who always curtsied to the new moon or turned their money at the first sight of a new one, and thought that bad luck would surely befall the person who saw a new moon through a window—unless the viewer went straight out and flung salt over the left shoulder. This should always be done if you spill salt and the old saying,

> *Spill salt for sorrow,*
> *Spill sugar for joy.*

is still believed by some country folk.

Very good luck would come to the person who saw a dapple-grey horse. Catch sight of his tail and your good luck became bad—unless you wetted your finger with your tongue immediately and made a cross on the toecap of your boot.

Speaking and bowing to magpies was quite a common thing and to this day I still nod my head and politely say 'Good morning, Sir', when I catch sight of one.

May blossom was never taken indoors and holly never before Christmas Eve. And some people still think that having lilac indoors or white flowers of any sort will bring bad luck. Once I took a little posy of spring flowers to a woman who was ill in bed and her husband refused to take the flowers indoors until I had removed the snowdrops.

Village funerals were very simple affairs. The undertaker most likely had a motor hearse that conveyed the coffin to Church but the few mourners would walk, all wearing deep black. When our

Gran died our mother had to borrow a bicycle to get to the funeral. It was sixteen miles each way up and down hill through Cotswold country. I remember her sending my elder sister down to the village to Mrs. Fisher to ask if she could borrow her best black coat and hat to go in.

Villagers were like that. If they had anything to lend anybody worse off than themselves they would do so without any second bidding. When my young stepbrothers had to go to the Radcliffe to have their tonsils out, Mrs. Frank Townsend lent them a nice white shirt each to go in. She had a biggish family and was always sending for our mother if the children had anything wrong with them. She was a good mother but not one for home doctoring. 'What do you think's wrong with our Bern?' she'd say, eyeing one of her sons thoughtfully.

'Nothing 'as a good dose of physic won't put right,' our mother would reply. And one of us would be sent home to bring back 'Some of me special' as she called it.

Some of the older people had what they referred to as 'Me best black'. The men's were often their wedding suits, green with age, and smelling strongly of moth-balls. These would be kept for what were called 'High days and holidays and bonfire nights', but were really for weddings and funerals, christenings and church on a Sunday.

Some of the women, like Mrs. Fisher, had their

best black; not our mother though. She borrowed
again when our Gramp died a few years later. The
first brand-new coat that she had during her married
life was one I bought her during the last war. But
not having new clothes never bothered her; hers,
like most of ours, came from jumble sales—'better
quality than I could afford to buy new,' she'd say,
after picking up a worn Harris Tweed coat for 2s. 6d.

Living down the bottom end of the village was a
deaf and dumb woman called Sally Castle, and for
a few shillings Sally would unpick a faded second-
hand coat, and then make it up again on the wrong
side to fit one of us. Our mother could manage to
make all sorts of things on her hand-turned sewing
machine, but coats were a little beyond her. Our
stepfather used to make us things on the machine
too, and once, as a special treat, he bought some
cheap red velveteen and made us three girls a dress
each for Christmas.

Not every family in the village could afford a
clock, but then it didn't matter really, for there
were several ways by which the time of the day
could be reckoned. For one thing, old Mark used
to drive through the village at the same time every
day, winter and summer; folks reckoned he was
never a minute out. He drove a float, a sort of open-
backed cart, with a good trotting pony in the shafts,
and took the milk in huge churns from the farm

where he worked at Yelford to Witney station to catch the 'Lunon' train. Mark always stood while he was driving, near the back, the float slightly tilted with his weight and that of the churn, the reins held high in his strong hands. He looked for all the world like a proud Roman in a chariot, with his weather-beaten face and fierce eyes. The daily journey to the station must have been a real treat, for at least he had a glimpse of the outside world—and that was something the other farm workers at Yelford rarely had.

Although a clock could be set on the outgoing journey, sometimes Mark would be late coming back—he often had to run errands in the town for his employers or sell rabbits to the housewives in Ducklington. In his strange sing-song voice he would say to us, 'If yer Mother waants a rabbit I'll skin 'er one fer ninepence.' And we used to shout this to him and tease him as he tore by in his float.

Thursday was market-day in Witney, though the locals called it 'Hurdle Thursday' because of the hurdles that were set up in the market-place. And the sheep and things that the farmers brought in to sell would be put into the hurdled pens. It was a meeting place where whiskered, gaitered farmers prodded the animals for sale and chattered over prices with friends or joined them in the local for a hard-earned pint. On these days Mark's employers, two lady farmers, would drive their smart pony and trap from Yelford to Witney, bringing with them lovely half-pound pats of yellow dairy butter to sell to people in Ducklington and Witney.

Another way we knew the time, at least if the wind was in the right direction, was when the whistles blew in the blanket mills at Witney. First at eight o'clock, when the workers started; at 12.30

p.m. when it was dinner-time; at 1.30 p.m., calling the weavers back, and then at six o'clock when it was time to go home. And on a Sunday we always knew when it was getting on for dinner-time for Mr. Amos who lived near us, whether he had anything to carve or not, always walked over to the wash-house where he proceeded to sharpen their carving knife with a great, long, blue sharpening stone. We could hear the noise as he swiftly drew the blade over the stone. 'Ah,' our mother would say, 'must be one o'clock, old Bert's tiggling his knife up.'

And then again, if the wind was in the west, we could hear the whistle of the Bampton Flyer, a local name for the train that puffed to and fro on a single track between Witney and Fairford, calling at some of the small villages in between, including Bampton. In those days they pretty well ran on time. 'Best get back to work,' our stepfather would say. 'Just heard the flyer's whistle, must be two o'clock.'

Some of the old men had big weskit-pocket watches hung on chains that stretched across their chests. One even had sovereigns dangling on his. Ask them the time, and with one movement the fat watch was pulled out and the thumb automatically moved over the face, cleaning imaginary dust off. 'Ten o'clock by God's time,' they would say. The older people would have no truck with Will Willett and his daylight-saving bill. Not wishing to offend, one had to do a quick bit of arithmetic according to whether it was summertime or wintertime.

I suppose, on the whole, we at Ducklington were pretty well catered for one way and another. There were two tiny village shops and the milkman's, the church and the school, Baker Collis's and the travelling men. We also had Snobby Castle to mend the boots of those who were not clever enough to mend their own, and Brummy Edwards to cut our hair. Once, and once only, Mother sent Bern and Bunt down to him to have a penny haircut.

Brummy sat them on an old box out in the garden and went over their heads with a pair of mule shears, the same pair that he clipped his old mule and donkey with. I think Brummy must have been the originator of the crew cut. When the boys got back home our mother burst out crying. Their hair was cut so short they looked almost bald. She gathered them into her arms saying, 'If I have to gnaw it off myself you'll never go down there again. Look at them,' she said to one of the neighbours, 'they look like a couple of old men, all their lovely curls blowing about on Brummy's garden.'

'Missus,' Brummy said when she went at him about it, 'thas what folks comes to I for, to have thur hair cut, and I likes to give full value. Anyhow,' he added, 'it'll grow thick and strong now—a

head of hair's like a grass field: cut it off short an'
it'll grow all the better.' Brummy went on bragging
a little, 'I got what the papers calls "the monopoly",
thur yent nobody else in the village what can
manage the job besides I.'

But when our stepfather came on the scene he cut
all our hair. We had to kneel up in a chair while he
snipped away at our locks—'keep your blessed head
still, young Mollie,' he'd say to me, 'or we shall be
having pickled ear for tea tonight.'

A very handy man our stepfather was; night after
night he used to sit up mending our boots, tacking
leather onto the soles to keep our feet warm and
dry. He used to say that his iron foot, that was the
thing he slipped the boot or shoe onto so that he
could mend it easily, was worth a pot of gold to
him. It really must have saved us pounds and
pounds during the years when we were all at home;
always it seemed one or other of us needed our
boots mended.

He was something of an inventor too. He could
make a mincing machine out of a worn-out grandfather clock's inside, or a lathe from an old treadle
sewing-machine.

His one luxury when we were all small was a
melodion which he could play beautifully. Sometimes on summer nights he would sit outside the
house and go through all the tunes that he knew—
the wartime songs, the up-to-date ones, and the

dirge-like ones: 'Don't Go Down the Mine, Daddy' or 'Break the News to Mother'. Then he'd have a go at hymn tunes, sometimes singing as well, with young Ben, only about three at the time, joining in, knowing all the words too.

But from this happy-go-lucky singing man he changed over the years, becoming moody, staying out late and drinking. His pals thought he was a marvellous fellow, yet he had rows with us all and kept our mother short of money. For years I wondered why the rot had set in, but not until after he died did I know. Apparently our mother found out that he was more than friendly with a young widow at one of the pubs he called at. And that was that; she just never forgave him. Slowly, through the years, she grew further and further away from him and so did we children, not really knowing why.

THE fields around the village were our playground, almost our whole environment.

In spring, the flat green meadows that lay either side of the banks of the Windrush were filled with fat yellow kingcups; water bubbles or water buttercups were local names for them. And in two or three special places we searched for the rare fritillary, darting backwards and forwards to pick the lovely snake-like flower heads. Sometimes we would find a few white ones, but mostly they were speckled, pinky purple, and for a few weeks our schoolroom window-sills, set high in the building, were lined with tightly packed jars of them.

In fact most of the year the jam jars were filled with our gleanings. From early spring when we gathered our first yellow catkins, that spilled their pollen on our desks, until winter, when we dragged the lovely fluffy trailing plant called Old Man's

Beard (Traveller's Joy), from the hedges on our way to school.

And it was in these same fields that we found watercress in abundance, that is if Watercress Charlie hadn't got there first. This wasn't his

proper name—just one we had given him. And gathering these dark green leaves was the only job he seemed to do. What he did in the months when it was not considered fit to eat the stuff we never knew, for to country people watercress is only eatable when there is an 'r' in the month.

We would sneak down to the 'Meds', our name for these special fields, and start to pick the cress, and I'll bet we hadn't gathered much before Charlie would come skulking up the hedge and run us off, although he had no more right down there than we had. But while ours was for our own eating, Charlie's was for selling. He would bunch his up and stack it in his little home-made rush basket and take it up to Witney to one of the shops.

Another place down the 'Meds' we used to go to was Buffy's Raddum. This was a specially planted willow copse that belonged to Mr. Tremblin, the local basket maker. And the Raddum was where he got his willow for making shopping baskets, clothes baskets which women used to collect their washing in, cradles and other things. The slim willow sticks, which were stacked upright in bundles to dry, had to be cut just at a certain time so that they did not become brittle but remained supple and easy to handle. We really should not have got into the Raddum at all, but in that damp, low-lying ground the kingcups were always bigger and better than those in the surrounding fields.

When spring had really come and the warm sun had brought out more meadow flowers, we would pick baskets of cowslips so that our mother might brew some home-made wine. We used to keep some of the best blooms ourselves to make what we called a 'tisty tosty ball'. Taking off the main stalk we would bunch up the thick flower-heads together, tying them in the middle with wool, and this made a lovely soft sweet-smelling ball. Then for hours we would play a game called 'Tell me true', each girl tossing a ball in the air, keeping in time with this jingle—

> *Tisty tosty, tell me true,*
> *Who shall I be married to?*
> *Tisty tosty, cowslip ball,*
> *At my sweetheart's name you'll fall.*

Each of us had our own favourites where the boys were concerned and we'd chant them—Percy, Charlie, Jimmy, Tom, Billy, Frankie, Bob and Bert, and, strange as it seemed, the ball always managed to fall at the name we wanted it to.

A little later on in the year we gathered armfuls of moon daisy, ragged robin, bloody butchers (purple orchid), meadow-sweet, and bright yellow flags—always there were plenty of wild flowers for the picking.

Each summer when Pudney Wilsdon cut the grass in the field just over the road from where we lived, we knew it was time to take our tea outdoors. We would arrive home from school to find a mountain of bread and jam cut and stacked on a plate, and a great big white jug filled with hot, strong tea. 'Go on, off you go, the lot of you,' Mother would say, 'and stay out and play in Pudney's field till I call you.'

Carefully carrying the precious food, we would

file over to the hay field and make ourselves a house by scooping up armfuls of sweet-smelling hay, piling it up to make it look like a room.

Then we would pick thickish grasses from the sides of the field where the mower had failed to reach and make ourselves drinking straws. When all the food and drink had gone we would dismantle the house and throw the hay over each other, filling our hair with millions of hay seeds which also stuck to our sweating bodies. Whatever the farmer

thought when he saw what we had done to his neat rows of hay I don't know, but it was such fun.

'Let's make pea shooters,' someone would say, and we'd all make a dive for 'The Mound', a thick double hedge where the biggest, strongest pigweed grew. These hollow stalks made super pea shooters, but we didn't use peas—no—'azzies' were our gun fodder. We'd grab handfuls of the berries, not yet ripe, from the may bushes, and fill our mouths with them, and holding the pea shooter to our lips we'd blow the berries through, hitting anything and everything. I know I got a clip round the ear for taking a pot-shot at old Mr. Judd, stinging him in the face with a volley of azzies. 'You be too cheeky by half,' Mr. Judd said. 'All you Woodleys be the same.'

Tree-climbing was another pastime that we all enjoyed, and most of the girls could shin up a tree as quickly as any boy.

The hedgerows in summer were festooned with dog roses, honeysuckle and waywind (bindweed). From most of the summer flowers we would suck honey, holding tiny flowerets of clover, waywind and honeysuckle up to our lips, savouring the sweet, fragile taste.

Long days were spent just sitting and playing in the fields making buttercup and daisy chains, holding bright buttercups under each other's chins to test if we liked butter, or chewing the sharp tangy leaves of the sorrel plant. We made hideous noises by holding a blade of strong grass between the thumbs, pressing it to the mouth, and blowing hard; the result was earsplitting, and heard a mile away.

A KIND OF MAGIC

We would pluck scarlet poppies from the growing corn and make poppy dolls by turning back the petals, tying them down with a piece of grass, making a red-skirted dolly with one green leg.

And there was one certain grass that we picked and curled each other's hair with, resulting in a tight frizzy tangle. I know once my hair was in such a state after Alice Spindlow had curled it for hours that our mother in desperation cut it off as short as a boy's. There was another sort of grass with little seeds growing alternately up the stalk. With this we tried to find out what sort of man we were going to marry. As our fingers moved up the stalk touching each seed we would chant—

Tinker, Tailor, Soldier, Sailor,
Rich man, poor man, beggar man, thief

—hoping that the last seed on the stalk was 'rich man'.

The boys often made whistles from thin sticks cut from the elder trees. First they would scoop out the white pith, then cut holes along the wood, and this gave them a few notes. Ben, one of my stepbrothers, could play anything you would like to name on one, for they were as good as any tin whistle.

And where birds had at one time dropped the seed into the forks of the gnarled old willow trees that stood drunkenly along the banks of the river,

142

blackcurrants and gooseberries would grow. Perching precariously on a branch, we would gorge the fruit, often before it was properly ripe, while below in the rushes we would find wild duck and moorhens' eggs that we took home by the dozen. Our mother always cracked these into a basin first in case they were addled. They were strong and rich, with bright orange yolks. Nine or ten of these completely filled the frying pan and made us a nice nourishing tea.

Other days we pinched swedes and turnips from Parker's fields, first gnawing the skin off with our teeth. Then we sat down in the middle of the field and had a good feed, eating the small circle of swedes that surrounded us. Once Mr. Parker caught me turnip-pinching. Our mother had always drummed into us that if we were caught doing anything we shouldn't, we were not to run away, but stand our ground. So I stood there, watching Mr. Parker's long thin legs getting nearer and nearer, his face purple with rage.

'What du think you're doing then?' he bellowed.

'Just eating a turnip,' I answered timidly.

'Well,' he said, 'you tell your stepfather I want to see him. (This was the farmer that he did week-end work for.) 'And if you don't tell him I want to see him I shall let him know that I caught you pinching me turnips.'

But I never did tell him—I knew that I would have got a hiding for pinching and I don't think Mr.

Parker, for all his faults, ever split on me either. Mind you, if he caught us mushrooming or black-berrying or gathering crab-apples for jelly in his fields he would simply tip them out on the grass and send us home with empty baskets.

A short cut across his forty-acre field led to Gorsehill woods where we gathered primroses in spring and wild strawberries in summer, and filled our pockets with woodnuts in autumn; and where sometimes in later years Denis, the youngest, went poaching and brought back plump cock pheasants.

We lived in a limestone district so our river was well-stocked with crayfish. And in the late summer or early autumn the lads of the village would go off on dark nights with a lantern and lie on the bank by a deepish pool. Here they would set their buckets and bait, often a bit of smelly meat, and wait. You had to be very quiet and still; a slight shadow cast on the water, and the little beggars would scuttle off.

Our brothers used to go, bringing back dozens of the crab-like creatures. They would put them live into the big black saucepan to cook over the fire, a pot full of wriggling red things. Then we would all sit down and have a nice feed of these delicacies.

So many things that were part of our quiet life still remain in the mind. Once, always during the summertime, we paid an annual visit to Yelford.

Our mother usually took Kitty Moore with us. Kitty was a cripple girl who lived up the back, and the only way she could get about was if someone took her out in her bath-chair.

It was one of those two-wheeled wicker chairs with a small extra wheel in front, attached to a long handle which was held by the rider who guided the chair—it just needed someone to push. Kitty would have young Denis on her lap, with Ben riding at the bottom by her poor mis-shapen feet. We others trotted alongside, holding on to the bath-chair when we got a bit tired.

The object of going to Yelford each summer was because, in a disused garden, there were several gooseberry bushes. The trip took nearly all day—

it was over four miles each way. Several times on the journey we sat by the side of the road to rest on the cool grass. One trip I remember vividly.

We passed a few cottages on the way—two after we left Ducklington, and we called at both of them for a drink, greedily gulping the ice-cold well water. We knew the women at the cottages and our mother stopped to chatter for a while before we pushed on. 'We might drop in on our way back,' Mother called to Mrs. Shepherd as we set off down the dusty road.

When we reached the garden at Yelford we fell on to the gooseberry bushes like a swarm of locusts, stripping off all the fruit, filling our baskets, bags and stomachs, prickling ourselves to death with the sharp thorns.

That morning on our way through the village we had called at Baker Collis's and bought a crisp new cottage loaf. 'Come on, grub up,' Mother cried, pulling the bread apart with her fingers. Then she spread dripping on it, giving us each a chunk. Like manna from heaven it tasted as we lay sweating in the overgrown garden, gnawing at our food.

I never taste dripping without remembering that day. There were clumps of columbines and rambler roses, and a rosemary bush and lots of weeds and birds everywhere, and the hot sun bore down from a cloudless blue sky.

We played for a while in the ruins of the burnt-out cottage, pulling a few remaining stones from the walls, dropping them into the garden. Then it was time to start for home and the long walk back.

When we reached 'The Plantations' Mother cried, 'Look at all this rotten wood lying about!' So we rushed around picking up the chunky bits, piling them on to Kitty's lap, squeezing lumps between her and Ben. Suddenly we were all tired. 'Let's have a bit of a sing-song,' Kitty said. 'We'll sing everybody's favourite in turn,' and for a while our steps were light as we strode along, piping out 'It's a Long Way to Tipperary' and our mother's special. 'Keep Right On to the End of the Road'.

We reached the village. In the twilight the gardens looked luminous and beautiful. We trailed along the last half mile, quietly tired. Denis was fast asleep.

The night smells rose up from the cottage gardens as we passed—damp grass and middens, stocks and roses. The evening star winked from a westerly sky; it was the end of a lovely day.

The great event of making the Christmas puddings each year is another that is particularly vivid. Try as she would, our mother never managed to get all the ingredients together by the allotted time— Stir-up Sunday—the first Sunday in Advent, usually in late November. No, ours more often than not were cooked about two weeks before Christmas and were the loveliest I've ever tasted. The preparation often took days. Suddenly the great red earthenware pan was set on the table and little by little the ingredients were thrown in. There was no weighing or measuring, all just guess-work. One messy job we children had to do was to stone the raisins. We would sit up at the table with a basin of water near at hand so that our sticky fingers could be dipped in now and then. Otherwise, after the stones were taken from the fruit, they simply remained stuck on the fingers.

Our stepfather always bought a quart of old beer with which to mix the puddings. The mixture was never put into the basins until we had all had a stir and a wish, the younger children standing on a chair so that they might take part. We all had to have a taste of the uncooked mixture just to see if anything had been left out. 'Something's missing,' our mother would say, and we'd poke our fingers into the raw pudding and taste, gazing heavenwards, trying to decide what it was. One year it was nutmeg, another spice, and another time it was sugar. Then one of us would be sent rushing up to town to get whatever was missing.

MAGIC MOMENTS

The next day the copper in the old wash-house was filled up and the fire lit, and there the puddings would bubble and boil all day long, our mother continuously having to make up the fire and add more water as it boiled away.

One year a Mrs. Hathaway who lived in the Square cooked her puddings nice and early. Afterwards she tied clean, dry cloths over them and set them up on a high shelf in the kitchen. She had made eight, the first to be eaten on Christmas Day. Early on Christmas morning she climbed up to get one. The first basin was empty, although the cloth was still tied on neatly. She reached for the next—that was empty too. And so were all the rest. The culprits were two of her sons. They used to come in at nights after the others had gone to bed and over the weeks had completely eaten the half-cooked puddings.

The excitement of pancake day in our house had to be seen to be believed, for no other day in the year could we afford such luxuries. The fun began as soon as our mother brought her big wash-stand jug from the bedroom and set it on the kitchen table. Into it went a quart of skimmed milk that one of us had fetched from Sarah Clarke's, and several eggs from our own hens, all whipped up together with plenty of plain flour into a creamy frothy mixture.

A KIND OF MAGIC

A new frying pan—another annual event for the great day—and a pound of best lard to cook the pancakes in, and we were all set to begin. Our mother's face was flushed and happy, her hair untidily wispy as she bent over her task. The fire burnt fiercely, so that she had to hold the pan above the flames. As each pancake was cooked it was doled out to the members of the family in turn, according to one's age, the eldest first.

The room was filled with squealing and laughing as our mother skilfully tossed each pancake high in the air. Blue smoke rose from the boiling fat and there was a strong smell of lemon as she slipped the long-awaited treat on to each plate. At last it was Ben's turn, he was last-but-one on the list. He had waited patiently for almost an hour, and as she tossed the pancake mother cried, 'Whose turn is it this time?'

'Mine, mine,' Ben shouted excitedly, and he rushed forward, plate in hand, and tried to catch it as it came down—our mother tried to do the same thing. She gave him a quick shove and he went backside first into a bucket of water and she herself, slightly off balance, stumbled a couple of steps sideways on to the sleeping cat. The hot pancake landed right on top of the squealing animal who made a bee-line for the door. Someone rushed to open it and the cat streaked out, completely enveloped in the cooked batter.

MAGIC MOMENTS

'That's yours boy, go and get it,' Mother yelled to him above the din as Ben heaved himself up from the bucket; with water dripping from his trousers he rushed out into the garden. Minutes later he came back, stuffing lumps of fluff-covered pancake into his mouth, having cornered his quarry in the wash-house.

The incident only lasted a few moments but the memory of that particular night will never be forgotten by the family.

Village Activities

FILLED with untold energy we threw ourselves into the few village activities. We romped along from the fair to Harvest Festival, from Christmas to the parish tea, and so on through the year. Our eyes were filled with stars and our hearts light, for everything we did was an adventure. There was little or no money to spend, yet the joy of those simple, unforgettable affairs remains always.

The village green where the two-day fair was held was just near our house. On the Sunday before the fair we were up long before it was light, to watch the caravans 'draw on'. There were never more than eight or nine, but to us it seemed like a colourful, magical parade. The vans, all horse-drawn, were painted in exotic colours, with shiny brass water buckets and jugs hanging and clanging outside. Dozens of children were packed into the quite small caravans.

Sometimes one giant steam engine would come to the fair. We could hear the chugging and the rattling of the wheels roaring over the flint roads miles away, and a gang of us would rush up a couple of miles or more to meet it. Then we'd run behind until it reached the green; like the children of Hamelin we followed the mechanical pied piper.

The coming of a steam engine to the fair meant there would be more than just stalls—perhaps roundabouts, and once a set of chair-a-planes came. We had never seen these flying chairs before and were scared stiff of them; we younger ones couldn't be persuaded to go on them at any cost. Grown-ups offered to pay for the ride but we hung back, saying we should get chucked out. 'I should be frit tu death,' said Willy Weaver, and we nudged one another in our shyness and fear. When evening came some of the older lads took their girls on this tearing, swirling monster and we stood dumb-founded at their flying legs, and were greatly sur-prised to find that after a short ride they returned to earth none the worse.

If any of us could cadge or earn a penny it would most likely be spent on a breath-taking ride on the 'Gallopers'—those beautiful, galloping horses with gaping mouths and flaming nostrils. We would mount these gaily painted animals, hanging onto their necks as if they were fiery steeds. They were fixed to the roundabout with brass rods that looked like giant barley sugar sticks. And the organ with its colourful, stiff-jointed figures of men and women

who played cymbals, drums and bells, blared loud, lovely tunes:

> *I'm one of the nuts from Barcelona,*
> *I clinkety clonk,*
> *I cassidy blonk.*

or

> *I'm for ever blowing bubbles. . . .*

—tunes that we hollered and bellowed for months after the fair had gone.

We would stand, mouths watering, watching the gypsy women make the 'Claggum'. This was the name we called the cream and brown 'fair rock' that they sold for 1d. a lump. The women would sit crouched round an open fire, their faces grimed with smoke, stirring treacle and brown sugar in a big black saucepan. For ages they seemed to sit there stirring and talking and smoking clay pipes. When the Claggum, or 'teasing candy' as it was sometimes called, had reached the right consistency, it was tipped out onto a wooden board.

When it was cool enough to handle the gypsies would spit on their hands and start to 'tease' the Claggum, first by flinging it over an old hook that was fixed to the side of the caravan, then they would pull it out from the hook—like a huge hank of cream wool it looked—flinging it back over the hook time and time again. Somehow they managed to get a thick brown stripe all through the rock. As soon as the Claggum had been teased to the right length it was whipped off and slapped back onto the board. Then, wielding a huge knife, the women cut the rock up into lumps.

In the evening the naphtha lights round the stalls hissed and flared, lighting up coconut shies and hoop-la, casting weird shadows over the fairground. A gypsy who always came to Duck Feast was Mrs. Topper, a black-eyed, fierce-looking woman with two wild-looking sons. She had no coconut shies or hoop-la, but made her money by selling water squibs. She would set up a small table—on it was a bucket of water (drawn from our well), and a pile of small shiny tubes, not unlike toothpaste tubes.

She would fill these with water from the bottom end and skilfully twist the open end up tightly with a pair of pliers. These she would sell for a penny. Many a love affair was started or strengthened at Duck Feast—this was how the fellows showed their affection, by chasing the girl of their choice and generously squirting her down the neck with one of Mrs. T.'s squibs.

'Tigglers' were sold at the fair too; they were just a bunch of soft strings of coloured papers fixed to a cardboard handle. These were a more gentle way of 'getting to know you', but served much the same purpose as the water squib, and the girls raced round and round the vans squealing in protest, but longing to be caught.

One year Bern, the eldest of our family, and about
thirteen at the time, had earned and saved about
1s. 4d. to spend at the fair. He told us he had hid it
away where none of us would ever find it. On the
feast Sunday when the caravans had drawn on and
settled down to their short stay in the village, Bern
suddenly burst out crying. 'What's up with him?'
Mother said. He had hidden his money away in an
Oxo tin under a clod of earth on Chalky (the village
green), but a caravan, with two lurcher dogs safely
tied to the axle, had parked on the spot.

Bern mooned about the fair with nothing to
spend. Early on the Wednesday he was up before

anyone else—the caravans had moved out, and so had his treasure. The dogs had evidently smelled something and had scratched the tin out. He found it empty in some rushes near by.

Bonfire night was the next event, not that we had any fireworks, but we did go round the village and peer over the gardens of those who were well-off enough to have a few sparklers. And although many of the cottages were thatched I can never remember any of them catching fire. A precaution against this was a bucketful of water and a bit of cloth fixed to the end of a long pole kept outside at the ready.

Before we knew where we were it was time to go carol singing. Our mother wouldn't let us 'go plaguin' ' people until three or four nights before Christmas—not that there were many places to sing at. It was no good going to ordinary cottagers like ourselves.

Real carol singing was confined to 'The Big House' and a few large houses where the people lived who were much better off than most of us. With candles set in jam jars we would set off. At some of the places we just received 'kind'—mince pies or lovely sweet-smelling apples, hot soup, sometimes a little money. At one or two places our carol singing was a sort of ritual.

VILLAGE ACTIVITIES

One house we loved to sing at was the elderly Miss Holtoms', two spinster ladies whose lives were devoted to the church. Dressed in long full skirts they would swish along the cold stone passages of the house where they lived and invite us to step inside out of the biting wind. Our first carol always, for them, was 'While Shepherds "Washed"' and then 'See Amid The Winter's Snow'. The Miss Holtoms' mince pies were the best we ever tasted—all fatty and crumbly. 'We will tell the Rector how beautifully you sang,' they would call as we hurried down the dark drive. But our mouths were too full to answer.

Every year we had a wondrous Christmas party at school. It was given by Major Feilden and his wife. Trestle tables were brought from the parish room and were absolutely bowed down with food: thin bread and butter—you could put a slice straight into your mouth it was cut so fine—and lovely square chunks of dough and seedy cake made by Baker Collis.

We would fill ourselves to bursting point, then slyly sneak a piece of cake and slip it into our pockets so that our mother might share the treat with us, but like as not it would be a crumbly mess by going home time.

As well as the lovely feed, we had another treat. In the 'big room' was a most wonderful Christmas tree. It touched the ceiling it was so tall, and it dripped with toys, dolls and drums, books and games. It was lit with real candles and dressed with shiny baubles such as we had never seen before. Everyone in the school received a present off the tree.

Then some time in January another special event was held. This was more a grown-ups treat. I think you had to be at least fourteen before you could go. It was the Parish Tea, which cost a shilling. Men and boys all scrubbed clean, red-faced and shiny, their hair plastered down with tappaleen (water) and dressed in navy-blue best suits smelling strongly of moth-balls or lavender, would stand in shy groups at the back of the hall. Women and girls also in their best, hair crimped with curling tongs, stood about in gossiping groups. First of all there was dancing—this was where we learned the Lancers, the Veleta, The Boston Two Step and the ordinary dances. We would plague the older women to take us round—clumsy, gawky, great country girls we were too.

All the music both for the dancing and the 'turns' that came later was played by a Mrs. Fowler who would tirelessly thump away on the old upright piano. The thing was, there probably wasn't anyone else in the village able to play.

We certainly had our shilling's worth on those wonderful nights—for the ladies of the village had prepared sandwiches and cakes and urns of thick brown tea. But those turns that each year were performed by the same stalwarts are what I remember best—Shade Franklin—Charley Edwards—Albert Hickman—Claude Collis—these were the men who sang and joked and made us very happy—year after year after year.

Before the end of the evening we were all red-faced and sweating, though the only heat came from a tortoise stove. But it was the excitement and the dancing and the fun, and the fact that all through those cold winters we were stuffed with great suet puddings and potatoes and mountains of bread and dripping that must really have been our very salvation. And it was these annual events that bound us, as a village, tighter together—making our own fun, sharing and giving.

Sometimes there would be a school concert—weeks and weeks of practice were needed to get some of the children to walk on the makeshift stage, but on the final night, when the parish room was again packed to bursting point, we all excelled ourselves. Except once, when Mavis Killmaster forgot her words as she was rendering 'Some people love to fun and frolic'. She had a good voice and we were all rather envious of her.

Once, I remember, Percy Bayliss brought the house down in a Nativity Play by saying to Mary, 'Blessed art thou, for thou art highly flavoured,' although he didn't realize what he had said.

On these concert nights the Rector would sit in the front row, his plump body perched uncomfortably on the bench-like seats. He would clap eagerly at all our efforts and dab his eyes with joy at the end.

Sometimes in the summer Bible meetings would be held on Chalky, and although we as a family were 'church', we used to love to go to these open-air meetings that were organised by the chapel; camp meetings they were. Most of the crowd was made up of children—although one old chap used to say of these meetings, 'all the 'nominations will be there'. We would gather round, staring wide-eyed as the lay preacher ranted and raged about the sins of the world. These men would fling their arms about and gaze heavenwards, as if the vision was written up there in that summer sky.

Brother Irvings used to play a little squeeze box thing, a melodion some folks called it, and this provided the music for the hymn singing. We loved the hymns. It didn't matter how loud you sang—in fact everybody seemed to try and outdo one another in efforts to be heard. Not like church, where we sang in quite subdued voices and the Rector preached his sermon in a more dignified manner. Not that the feeling of the Lord was any less out on Chalky—it was just that we put more into it, and bellowed 'Jesus wants me for a Sunbeam' or 'At the Cross, at the Cross', loud into the summer evening.

The bigger boys, those who had started work, used to stand at the back of the meeting and would sing, quite loudly, parodies to the hymns—and when we got home we would sing them—only to get our ears boxed for taking the Lord's name in vain. The one that was sung to the tune of 'At the Cross' ended like this:

> *They were eating currant buns,*
> *When they heard the German Guns,*
> *And the bottom of the bucket rolled away.*

But the really rude part came before that.

In the summer we had another school treat. This one was always held on the rectory lawn—the same

trestle tables would be carried from the parish room
—the same lovely wafer-thin bread and butter and
Doughy Collis's cakes. After tea some of the children
from the top class would give a display of country
dances. I wasn't often chosen to dance because I was
big and clumsy and probably Miss Spencer, our
teacher, thought that I would not be able to produce
the white dress and plimsolls that were required for
those taking part in the dances.

But one year I assured her that I had a white frock
to wear—really, it was the one my sister had worn
when she was confirmed. My mother declined to
have me confirmed because of my tomboyish and
unruly behaviour—but I could wear the dress.
White lawn it was, with white embroidery on, and
the edge of the skirt was scalloped, but as it was
several sizes too big for me this lovely scalloped
piece didn't show because of the huge hem my
mother had put on it. Never mind, I was going to be
able to do 'Rufty Tufty' and 'Gathering Peasecods'
with the rest.

But first we all sat down to eat. Mrs. Edwards
came round with a big white enamelled jug full of
hot strong tea. She was just pouring some out for
me when Chris Goodwin shoved his great arm across
to grab the last bit of cake on the plate, and sent the
jug flying out of poor Mrs. Edward's hand. The
tea went all over me and the white lawn frock.
When it came to dancing time Miss Spencer eyed

the big brown stain on my frock and 'tut-tutted' and said, 'You can't possibly dance in front of the Rector looking like that—Nellie Clark can take your place.' How I hated Nellie Clark as she simpered through those dances while I sat and sulked.

Never mind, I had my own back later when we ran races, three-legged, sack, and just ordinary fast running. I beat her every time and went proudly home with eightpence winning money—but had a darned good hiding for spoiling the frock.

The only other big events were the Harvest Festivals held at the church and chapel, both lovingly decorated year after year.

The church were first to hold theirs—the almost bare sanctuary suddenly sprang into life, stooks of wheat greeted us as we entered, outsized marrows filled the windows, onions, leeks and apples were heaped on every ledge, great bunches of Michaelmas daisies and giant dahlias nodded from earthenware jugs, and an unusual crowd filled the pews. The Rector preached of 'my faithful few', those stalwarts who attended always. 'I thought he was quite rude,' Mother said, but turned up just the same next Harvest Festival.

We looked forward to the chapel one, at least to the sale of produce held on the Monday. We would get there early, completely filling the front seats. Of course we had no money and gazed open-mouthed as people passed over a few pence for cabbages and apples, carrots and pears.

Always in pride of place was a beautiful loaf of bread, much larger than the ones we had at home, and all down the middle, and running along the top, it had a pattern of wheat ears, shiny, golden and brown. Placed on either side of the big loaf were several minute cottage loaves—this was our interest because dear, hunchbacked Mr. Irvings always bought these little loaves and distributed them amongst us. We never waited until we got home to eat them, but stuffed them into our ever-hungry mouths as soon as he gave them to us.

Just before Easter we children made a pilgrimage to Gorsehill Woods to gather primroses to help decorate the church, bunching them up with the pale green leaves, tying them carefully with wool. Then the Miss Holtoms would place them lovingly round the font and surround them with tangy moss.

This was our small contribution. There was never any money to chink into the plate that Mr. Spindlow brought round as the last hymn was being sung, although when we got a bit older we used to pretend to put something on there, but he knew we didn't—there was the absence of that chink as the pretended money failed to land. But I don't suppose that the dear Lord thought any the worse of us for that.

Our beloved Rector at Ducklington was the

Reverend Tristram. He was an ideal village parson and was kindness itself to the villagers. There was a little charity money that he gave out to the poor but our mother often told us that he gave much of his own money away too. 'There's some people for ever in and out of that rectory just for what they can get from him. Not good Christian folk neither. Still,' she'd go on in her independent voice, 'nobody can ever say as I've had a penny charity money. My father used to say to me "Ah my girl, an independent woman an' a beggar's purse en't worth a curse"; perhaps it isen't but it's a nice feeling inside.'

Most mornings the Rector came into the school, sometimes taking us for scripture lesson. He had been educated at Magdalen College, Oxford, and taught us the correct way to pronounce it (Maudlen). It was his idea to have an ancient barn converted into the parish room, and this is still the only meeting place in the village. He started a reading room there too, and got Miss Polly Holtom to run the lending library.

Old Mr. Hill who lived up the other end of the village, near the milkman's, used to toddle right down to get a book for himself and his ailing wife. One day Miss Polly was trying to help him choose a book and said to him in her high-pitched, educated voice, 'Oh Mr. Hill—have you ever had *A Night Out*?' 'Yes Miss,' Mr. Hill replied cheekily,

'I've had several,' and everybody burst out laughing; Miss Polly moved quickly from the fiction to the history shelf.

At the Rector's suggestion a girls' club was formed. You had to be between ten and fourteen to be able to join. It was held in the parish room every Thursday and the fee was 2d. a week. We learnt folk dancing and acted little plays and did what we called exercises (P.T.) or just played organised games. I did not join until I was twelve and then was only allowed to because Bern, Bunt and Betty went to choir practice on that night and I could go and come back with them.

Characters and Neighbours

Edna

APART from the two-day annual fair, and Christmas, Harvest Festivals and the Parish Tea, nothing spectacular happened in Ducklington. But the place was full of lively characters who brought colour and sometimes excitement into our otherwise quiet rural lives.

There was Edna—poor Edna—subject to fits and 'the drink'. She was tall and thin and had a pile of black hair above her blotchy purple face. Her eyes were wild and bulbous and we kids were all scared stiff of her, and squittered past the tall stone wall that circled the house where she lived.

She would career round the village on her old bicycle, searching for anyone who would get her a

170

bottle of spirit. From somewhere she would get the money. The landlords of the two pubs had been warned not to serve her but she'd hang about till she found a willing passer-by. Sometimes Edna would wait in vain for her bottle while one of the villagers sat in the ale bar of The Bell, supping away at Edna's expense.

We came upon her one hot sunny day; she was sprawled out under one of Pudney Wilsdon's sweet-smelling hayricks—tight as a tick she was. Her shiny black straw hat askew, her face more purple than ever and her loose red mouth wide open. Perhaps she was dead; we stood and stared at her. Then she started to grunt and snore like a pig.

Suddenly she opened her eyes and saw four ragged children staring at her. With one movement of her long thin body she was up. Swinging her empty bottle high above her head she chased us over the meadow. Her blood-curdling screams brought a farm worker to our rescue.

'I'll drown myself,' Edna shouted, 'I'll jump in the river.'

'Go on then, jump!' Carter Temple said, but she didn't. This was an old trick of Edna's to threaten drowning when she was caught drunk.

Someone sent for her father and Edna slunk home, shame-faced. At other times she would let down her hair and ride round and round the village on her bicycle, shouting at anyone who went by, and only go back home when she was utterly exhausted.

The old man who lived next door to us, in the thatched house, was always known as 'e in the corner. Go out on any starlight night and 'e in the corner would be standing by the gate, one eye shut tight and the other pressed to an ancient telescope.

'Venus is clear tonight,' he would say if we happened by. 'She won't be as near again for a thousand years.' We should have listened more intelligently to him.

CHARACTERS AND NEIGHBOURS

One night 'e in the corner spied something special in his telescope. Excitedly he shouted, as if he were greeting the heavenly body, 'Jupiter, Jupiter!' and a small voice from the darkened roadway replied, 'No it isn't, Mr. Horne, it's me, Claudie, Claudie Collis.'

By trade 'e in the corner cut and carved names on tombstones. Lying abed we could hear him chipping away in the outhouse, carving sweet verses to lost villagers.

Whether someone had cancelled an order or whether 'e in the corner laid in a stock at some time I don't know, but for months a plain tombstone was propped up against our gate (the three cottages used the same). On the tombstone was fixed a notice that read 'For Sale for Four Pounds', but who on earth in our village had four pounds!

When 'e in the corner fell ill, our mother used to pop in and do his housework for him or take him some hot pudding or stew. One day in early summer it was, he said to her, 'Missus, stop they dratted birds a-singing, they gets on me nerves, chirp, chirp chirping away all day long.' The thick thatch of his snug cottage was full of sparrows and the garden full of blackbirds and thrushes greedily gorging his fruit. 'Poor old fellow,' our mother said. 'He's complaining about the birds singing—where he's going there'll be no bird song.' The next day 'e in the corner died.

A KIND OF MAGIC

Everybody liked Dick Clarke. Dick would have been called a spastic these days. Poor devil!—legs mis-shapen, bent inwards at the knees, and hands and fingers all knotted up. He shuffled about somehow on two sticks, dragging his feet along the ground. He lived with his brother and sister. The brother was our postman and he also kept a few cows. And each day Dick would prop himself up in their little shed which they used as a dairy and turn the handle of the milk-separating machine; this would take him about a couple of hours to do.

But he was cheerful and chatty, and he would tease us girls about boys. There wasn't much that went on that Dick didn't know about.

Young lads of the village were always on the lookout to make a few coppers, my brothers amongst them.

Some of them would make themselves a little wooden truck by using the wheels off an old pram and a box cadged from one of the shops in the town. Then they would go round the village roads picking up horse manure.

All you needed for this job was a truck, a small shovel and a good left foot. The foot was placed behind the heap of muck, and with the shovel in the right hand you had to take a sharp shove at the heap so that you collected all the muck at one go without scattering it all over the place. This the lads would sell for about sixpence for a full truck. Those who hadn't a truck did their collecting in an old bucket. And gathering up the horse manure as they did helped our roadman Charlie Hickman who had a long length of road to keep clean and tidy—nearly seven miles, which included Ducklington. To me Charlie had always seemed aged, a weather-beaten, gnarled old fellow who rode an old black tricycle. He used to carry his tools tied on the back of his

trike and these included a broom, shovel, scythe, sickle, fagging hook and sharpening stone, besides his dinner bag and an old coat. He always wore thick brown cord trousers yorked up below the knee with leather straps, and his face was the colour of a bit of old leather.

When we went back to school on some days Charlie would be sitting on the side of the road eating his victuals—usually a great hunk of bread and fat bacon. This was always swilled down with a bottle of cold tea, winter and summer. We used to kick at the neat little piles of dust that he had carefully swept up. 'Drat your eyes on you, you little devils. I'll swipe you with me broom handle if I catch you,' he'd yell as we ran away.

Besides doing the hard road-work Charlie kept bees and pigs at home and hand-planted three of his allotments each year with barley, tilling the soil with a breast plough. Then he would cut the corn with a scythe and take it to the flour mill in the village to be ground. This barley meal was to feed and fatten up his pigs. Then Charlie was given notice to quit his job, just a month off his eightieth birthday. We had other road-men but Ducklington never seemed quite the same without the old man's familiar figure.

There was a family of eight who lived fairly near us. They all grew up great strapping people, yet when they were tiny their furniture consisted of orange boxes to sit on, and one big deal table to eat from. When the Rector went to visit them he was asked to take a seat—on the stairs.

Yet no one thought them any the worse for this. They were clean and healthy and lived mostly on 'taters, bacon and greenstuff. The father worked hard and his allotments were a picture, and woe betide anyone who put a foot near them. He was a strong, red-faced, giant of a man who could push a breast plough as easily as most men push a wheelbarrow. Rabbits invaded his allotments from the surrounding fields, sneaking his precious greenstuff. But he would set traps for them and made a fair bit on the side. Most of the housewives gladly gave him ninepence for a rabbit.

A man we were scared stiff of was called Peter Painter, who lived in the town near by. He was an expert at biting off puppies' tails. He was never seen without a pail with a lid attached, always shut too. As kids we thought this was full of bitten-off tails. Mothers would say to disobedient children, at least to the little boys, 'If you be naughty I'll send for Peter, an' 'e'll do the same fer you as 'e does to they puppy dogs.' And for a while the boys would behave and look very solemn at the prospect of their 'belongings' being whipped off and carted away in Peter's lidded pail. We found out when we were older that his pail contained pigs' chitterlings, probably given him in lieu of payment for biting off the puppies' tails.

Another man we were frightened of was Joey the Flag. He pushed a little old truck round the town filled with something mysterious, all wet and wriggling. The truck was partly covered with a sack which dripped and made a trail in the road as he went by. We were almost afraid to look as he scuffled along—you could hear the contents of the truck, flip-flop, flip-flop, as he passed. Mothers used to threaten naughty children by saying that they would get Joey to push them under the sack and take them away. We found out that he, like Peter, was carrying pigs' chitterlings around. Joey used to collect them from a slaughter-house and take them to a large piggery on the other side of the town, where, people said, they were fed back to the pigs.

There was never any real tragedy in the village. The worst thing that happened was when foot and mouth disease struck Wilsdon's farm. One morning we went to school to find disinfectant pouring over the road. The farm buildings happened to be on both sides of the village street.

The slaughter of the animals came first. All the farmers' men were sent out into Gooseham field where they had to hand-dig a great deep pit. The bottom was lined with cartloads of faggots and paper. Then the bodies of the cattle were thrown in —I still remember seeing that huge pile—stacks of legs, tails, heads and bodies piled up against the sky line. They set fire to the lot and the awful smell of burning flesh floated over our village for days. After the fire had done its job the workmen poured sacks and sacks of quicklime on the remains, and the hole was covered over with turf. And although there were two other farms very close, the outbreak was confined to Wilsdon's.

At the back of the row of cottages where we lived there was another row of three or four. Joe Hill and his wife lived 'up the back'. They were very old; Mrs. Hill died there. Old Joe must have been well over seventy. He lived on there for a while longer, then he fell ill. Neighbours did what they could but in the end old Joe was taken off to the nearest work-house.

And one fine morning someone came and put their bits of furniture out into the yard, and along came a man and sold it. There was a white scrubbed table, and a few kitchen chairs and odds and ends. Most of the items were bought by the nearest neighbours. Our mother paid four shillings for what was probably the most prized possession in the cot-tage, Joe's wooden armchair.

At some time Mrs. Hill had crocheted the red woolly cover that was fixed over the spars at the back to stop the draught getting on Joe's shoulders. We used 'Joe Hill', the name we gave the chair, for years at home. I have it now; the wooden arms are almost white with wear—the crocheted cover has long since worn out and has been replaced by a bright red cushion, and we still call it 'Joe Hill'.

In those days the work-house was the only place for the very old, especially if they were ill and had no relations. By selling the bits of furniture these unfortunate souls could at least have a decent burial —to have to end one's days in the work-house was dreadful, but to have a pauper's grave was much worse.

What some of the really old folks suffered from was semi-starvation. One dear old lady that our mother used to go to see almost lived on what she called 'tea-kettle broth'. This was a piece of dry toast soaked in hot water—no wonder some of them folded up like flowers at eventide and died.

Growing Pains

I CAN remember the excitement and indeed the sadness, when our sister Betty went off to service—somewhere in Hampshire it was, but it seemed like the other side of the world to us. When girls went to be servants in big houses, their future mistresses would send a list of clothes that the young girls needed. Mothers had to find two of everything, and all had to be marked with the owner's name.

Our mother had such a list and wondered how on earth she was going to get together the necessary items. But the neighbours were wonderful; one made a morning apron, another made two white cambric nightgowns, lace-edged and feather-stitched. And dear, deaf-and-dumb Sally Castle made a morning and afternoon dress and never charged a penny for the making.

They came to fetch our sister in a car. This was wonderful because at that time only two or three people in the village had such a luxury. This one was chauffeur-driven, so we knew that the family must have pots of money. But we all cried when she rode away—a forlorn figure she made. This was the first time any member of the family had gone away to work. But one fourteen-year-old out of the house left a bit more room for those that were left.

With her leaving, my elder sister's jobs became mine, and those that I had done became my step-sister's. So now, before I went to school, ashes had to be taken up and sifted, and the black grate given a bit of a shine. One of my brother's daily tasks was to get the morning's wood. Every night found him up the hedgerows gleaning dry twigs and little pieces of rotten wood at the base of the hedge; box wood was unheard of. In winter time he would slip the kindling wood into the fire-oven so it was nice and dry by morning. Then it would light easily and boil a kettle so that he might have a cup of tea before he went off to work.

But our mother was rather extravagant with wood and loved to have what she called a 'blizzy'. Many times Bunt, stumbling from sleep about six o'clock on a winter's morning, came downstairs to find his precious kindling wood had gone. Our Mother had burnt the lot. 'Had one of my blizzies, boy, had to warm myself up a bit before I went to bed,' she would say when Bunt chided her. And he would have to go and get some more sticks, prob-ably damp ones. Then he would kneel in front of the grate and blow himself red in the face in an effort to get the wood to catch.

My Saturday job was to scrub the stone-flagged
back kitchen, a job I detested. Once, at Christmas-
time, our stepfather brought home a couple of ducks,
and our Mother quickly made a bargain with me.
'I'll do your scrubbing,' she said, 'if you'll go and
pick the ducks.' I was out in that old wash-house for
hours and hours; those ducks had half-a-dozen coats
on, I'm sure. The trouble was I did not know that

the art of picking ducks is to plunge the thumb and
finger right into the thick down as near to the skin as
possible. After being out in that freezing wash-
house for about three hours, cold and miserable,
crying, and covered in feathers, I gave up, though
the ducks still had quite a bit of fluff on them, but I
didn't care. The weekly scrubbing of the back
kitchen never seemed so bad after that.

Bunt, the more enterprising of my real brothers,
used to earn himself a bit extra by catching moles.
He would set his traps in Pudney's field, and early
every morning he would go out to collect those he

had caught. Then he would skin them and carefully tin-tack the velvet-like skins on a board to dry. When he had got a dozen or more he would take them up to Warburtons in the town, where he would get sixpence each for them.

A KIND OF MAGIC

Both Bern and Bunt helped on a milk round before they went to school. In the very cold weather they wore old socks on their hands in an effort to keep them warm. Handling a steel can on a frosty morning could be murder. They got sixpence each a week for this, a seven-day week at that. But they got a few 'perks' as well: housewives would give them hunks of cake and apples, or perhaps a copper or two at the end of the week.

When Bunt left school he worked for a few months for the milkman, his wages being half-a-crown a week, but he used to wear out that amount in shoe leather. So, as soon as he could, our stepfather got him a job at the brewery where he worked and Bunt stayed there, rising to the job of yard foreman until he was called up during the war.

Bern, the eldest, was already holding down quite a good job at one of the big warehouses in the town, where they finished off and packed the blankets and despatched them all over the world. He was lucky to get a job like this because during the 1920s good jobs were few and far between. When he had first left school he worked on the farm for Mr. Parker, walking up to Barley Park Farm at seven in the mornings, taking a short cut across the forty-acre field. Then our mother heard of this job going at the warehouse and walked up to Witney and got it for him.

Some Sunday mornings after he started work, Bern would say, 'Pop up to Smith's and get a few sweets.' Mrs. Smith was a widow who lived in one of the cottages 'up the back' and she sold sherbet dabs, cheap toffees and liquorice pipes in her front room. Armed with sixpence we would rush up there with strict instructions on how to spend it. Two penn'orth of toffees at two ounces a penny—hard as a brick but very welcome. Six ha'penny gob-stoppers, one each for us younger ones and one each for Bern and Bunt. We loved gob-stoppers; they were so big you could hardly move them from one side of your mouth to the other, and as you sucked away at them they kept changing colour—we would fetch them out of our mouths, saying 'mine's pink now, mine's yellow'. Then we had to get two penny bars of Cadbury's chocolate for our parents and a ha'-penny bag of popcorn with the last copper. We would hang round Bern until he had shared the popcorn with us and had doled out each a toffee. And that was that—everybody had had a treat but the remaining toffees were his.

We loved it when our Auntie Emily came home for her annual holiday. She was a lady's maid to someone very wealthy, and she nearly always gave us some money to spend. Once she met Mick and I in the square at Ducklington and gave us sixpence each—sixpence each!—we were practically millionaires.

A KIND OF MAGIC

We went into the village shop and spent thre'-
pence each. I bought two sherbet fountains and
forty aniseed balls (twenty a penny). Instead of

sucking up the white powder through the liquorice
tube I just emptied the whole packet down my
throat. Suddenly the sherbet started to fizz and
bubble and pour out of my mouth and down my
nose. Red-faced, eyes watering, I coughed, splut-
tered and nearly choked to death outside Stranges'
farm. 'Greedy guts,' were the only words of sym-
pathy that I got from Mick who had her mouth
chock-full of nougat.

We had planned to tell our mother that Auntie
Emily had in fact only given us thre'pence each.
We went home and told our tale and handed over
the money. Then, wallop! we were punished for
telling lies. Our *dear* aunt, in the meanwhile, had
called at our house and told our mother what she

had so *generously* given us. We were sent off to bed
for the rest of the day, but I didn't mind so much
because I still had the remaining aniseed balls stuck
up my knicker leg.

Pig Killing

OUR parents, like many of the village folk, kept a couple of pigs—'ran a couple of pigs' was the expression. Much of the food they ate was 'come by', apart from the toppings (pig meal). After school in summertime we would go off with hessian sacks and fill them with sow thistles, dandelion leaves, keck (cow parsley) and waywind. The pigs loved this fresh-picked food.

Little pig 'taters were boiled up in an old saucepan over the living-room fire every day. These were mixed with a little toppings and the water our own vegetables had been cooked in, to make a good evening meal for the animals. Keeping pigs meant there was no waste at all for they cleared up cabbage leaves, rotten apples and garden weeds, and provided a good supply of manure for gardens and allotments.

In the autumn we paid an annual visit to a field a couple of miles away called 'The Devil's Nutting Ground' where there were several giant oak trees in the field and in the hedge. Here we collected acorns by the peck. When these were fed to the pigs it was almost guaranteed to put a couple of extra inches of fat on their backs before it was time to kill them.

Then, about the middle of October when the weather had turned colder, our stepfather would go down to the village and ask Piggy Humphries to come and kill them. One we would have indoors for eating, the other Mr. Humphries would buy, and the money we got for it paid Baker Collis what we owed him for toppings and bought us a few warm clothes for the coming winter.

The pig killing now seems to have been a gory affair, but it was such a common occurrence in the village that we took no notice at all.

Mr. Humphries would arrive on his bicycle with his tools carefully wrapped in a sack: a pig sticker, a very long sharp knife, and a sharpening stone. The poor animals seemed to sense that something was wrong and while the men struggled to slip a

noose over each snout to help drag them out of the
sty ready for the killing, they would set up such a
squealing that could be heard all over the top end of
the village.

Once the animal was outside, the men would lift it
on to the rough bench; then Mr. Humphries would
plunge his pig sticker down the animal's throat,
cutting an artery; the blood used to ooze out. Some
people made a point of catching the blood in a basin.
This, mixed with other ingredients, makes very
good black puddings.

Once the pig was dead the carcass was placed on a
pile of smouldering straw to burn off the bristles.
Then, re-sharpening his already sharp knife, Mr.
Humphries skilfully cut up the carcass. Our mother
would be standing close by with a couple of dishes
and a clean bucket for the chitterlings. Onto the
dishes went the heart, liver, kidney and head. And
my elder brothers waited patiently for the bladder
which they used for ages afterwards as a football—
the only sort they ever possessed.

Then the flear—that's the piece from which the
home-made lard is produced, was hung up in the
cool wash-house along with the lights. Then the
'sperib' (spare rib), hams and backbones were cut
out, leaving two sides. After treatment these sides
would be our winter's bacon.

The first night's supper after a pig had been
killed was the best treat in the world. That was

when we had the pig's fry: the liver and fat fried in plenty of lard. Two loaves of bread we would eat with this, wiping our plates round so as not to leave a morsel on them.

All the offal and the 'sperib' had to be eaten quickly in case it went off. Sometimes the weather would suddenly turn very mild. Then we had to gorge like mad so as not to waste a thing, and for about a week we all lived like fighting cocks, stuffing ourselves with great boiled heart and kidney puddings and wonderful faggots that our mother made from the lights, tongue and sweet herbs. She would cover each faggot with a small piece of the caul, the lacy portion of fat that protects the intestines.

Another thing we would have was 'Boney Pie' made from the backbones that Piggy Humphries cut out when he carved up the carcass. The 'sperib' we always had on pig-killing Sunday, baked in the coal fire oven along with huge, crisp, fatty potatoes.

After soaking the head and trotters in salt water for a couple of days our mother would set about making the most wonderful tasty brawn. 'Collared head' is the real country name for brawn. She would boil the head and trotters in fresh water along with half-a-dozen good-sized onions, a few peppercorns and a blade of mace, until the meat fell off the bone. The meat was then put on to a large dish and chopped very finely, and to this was added a cup of chopped sage, pepper to taste and a teaspoon of nutmeg, and some of the liquor which the meat had been boiled in, making the mixture quite wet and floppy—wetter than cake mix. While it was still warm it was put into greased basins with a plate on the top and something very heavy on the plate to press the brawn well down. When it was cold and turned out it was all set firm and could be cut into slices.

Then there were the chitterlings to clean. First they were turned inside out on a stick to get them clear of any waste matter. This was quite a hard job and messy, too, with no tap-water available. Then they were left to soak in salt water for three days. Our mother would plait the tiny ones and simmer them all until they were tender. We would either eat them cold or frizzled up in the frying pan.

The day after the pig killing we kids would sit round the table and help to cut up the flear into pieces about as big as a meat cube. This was put into saucepans over a gentle heat. As soon as the fat started to run it had to be poured into basins so as not to let it boil away; you had to keep at it all the while. 'Pop out and pick me a sprig of rosemary,' Mother would say to one of us. This gave the lard a wonderful flavour. (She always put rosemary in milk puddings too.) After melting down all the flear we would have four or five basins of snow-white lard. This would last us on our bread for weeks and weeks.

Then the little bits of shrivelled-up cooked fat which was over from the lard-making made us another tasty meal. We called them 'crutlings' though in some counties they are known as 'scratchings'. We ate these piping hot, straight from the pot—it was a sort of reward for helping to cut up the flear.

Another job that had to be done quickly was the salting and pickling of the sides and the hams. Out in the back kitchen where it was cool our stepfather would set up his salting trough by standing it on a couple of trestles. He would place the sides in the trough and rub salt and saltpetre well into the meat, turning it over in the brine every day so that it was all well-salted. After several days of this treatment the bacon was taken out of the brine and hung up to dry off, either on racks near the ceiling or behind a door, carefully covered with a bit of butter muslin. Then in a little while it was ready for eating.

Sometimes our stepfather would salt the hams like the bacon, but at other times he pickled them in a mixture of old beer, brown sugar, juniper berries and salt. He would boil these up together and when the mixture was cold it was rubbed into the hams every day for a month. Then the hams, like the bacon, were hung up to dry off. 'Best pictures we got in the house,' Mother would say to visitors.

The flavour of ham pickled like this was wonderful and something I have never tasted since. While it lasted we used to have a slice each on Saturday nights for supper, cut thick and fried in plenty of lard. They were such great slices that one filled a good-sized dinner plate.

Pigs were often twenty score and over—the 'fatter the better' the women would say; the meat was more flavoursome and satisfying anyhow. During the winters we had the bacon cooked all sorts of ways—fried, great lumps boiled and eaten hot or cold, and about once a week we had a great big bacon and onion clanger. That's what we called the huge roly-poly that our mother made from flour paste, butcher's suet, chunks of bacon and thickly sliced onions, all rolled up and sewn into a floured cloth. It was about a foot long and bubbled and boiled in the oval saucepan for about five hours.

One very large family in the village had one of these bacon and onion clangers every day—while the children were all small—and because of this they earned themselves the nickname of 'Clanger' Browns, to distinguish them from several other families of the same name.

GOOD TIMES and BAD

OUR mother's temperament blew hot and cold according to the weather or the domestic situation. Sunny days found her full of the joys of spring, light-hearted and loving, taking us for miles, pushing a pram full of kids on wooding jaunts, blackberrying or mushrooming, or just out in God's good air. No doubt there were occasions when she was very hard up, or maybe just fed up with everything in general. At times like this you had to watch out—slap bang! —you would be smacked for the most trifling thing.

Once I called a boy a 'guts', and she rubbed carbolic soap in my mouth—to wash out the filth, she said—and I sat on the stairs for ages picking that soap out of my teeth. One thing she could not abide was any sort of swearing, or rough words, and although we were surrounded by people who spoke what she termed as 'a bit on the rough side', we were all encouraged to speak properly.

When we became too big for hidings our mother punished us by sending us up to bed without any tea. In the summer, when all the other children were out at play, this was a worse punishment than a good hiding. I don't think any other members of the family were sent off to bed as often as I was, but then none of them happened to be as wilful and cheeky.

But one of our mother's favourite sayings (and

she had got one for most occasions) was: 'Never let the sun go down on your anger', and often when I had been sent to bed early she would bring me up a plate of bread and dripping just as it was getting dark, and sit on the bed and talk to me while I ate it. Then she would give me a goodnight kiss and ask me to try to be a good girl the next day. 'And don't forget to say your prayers,' she would call as she went back downstairs, 'and ask the dear Lord if He can make you behave, because I can't.'

Every night in wintertime our mother would fill the oil lamp and trim the wick. Then she would clean the glass chimney by pushing her duster up the fine clear glass, blowing on it and then polishing it to make it shine so that it would give out a better light.

After we had all had a good hot meal and the crocks were washed up and stacked away, the big table was left clear for us to play for a while before going off to bed. For hours we girls would make doll's furniture from conkers—the lovely shiny horse chestnuts made a good base for chairs and tables. Carefully selecting the squat ones we would stick them with pins or spent matches to act as legs, using some as frames for the backs of the chairs and sofas, weaving wool in and out to give a nice up-holstered effect. Sometimes a table could be made from a good big fat conker.

Empty match boxes were carefully saved and by

gluing them together, three high and two across, we made a lovely chest of drawers using big-headed pins to act as handles to open each box-like drawer.

Other winter evenings were spent doing french knitting. For this you needed an empty cotton reel with four tin-tacks nailed on to one end. These tin-tacks acted as needles really, on which were set four stitches. Any odd bits of wool were used. Then, holding the reel in the left hand and a pin in the right, you kept slipping the stitches over the tin-tacks, gradually pulling the knitting, which was tubular, through the cotton reel hole. Yards and yards of this we did, sewing it up afterwards to make pretty mats for our mothers to stand pot plants on. Some girls even made fronts of cushion covers with it.

Another indoor game that we played for hours was 'I spy with my little eye'. Once my brothers and some village lads were playing this game when a fellow called Sid said he spied something beginning with L.L. They tried for ages to guess what began with L.L. and finally all the gang said 'Give it up'. Then Sid announced very proudly 'Lectric Light'—it was a battery torch one of the lads had on his bicycle. He was never allowed to forget this and is still referred to as 'Old Lectric Light' by fellows who were there.

We often got hold of the wrong end of the stick because we didn't speak or pronounce our words properly. 'Our Father Giraffe in heaven,' I said for years when repeating the Lord's Prayer, and 'God in heaven save my "soup" ' instead of my 'soul'. And for years I puzzled my brains as to where the Darden Hills were. I knew the Aston Hills were just outside the village on the way to Aston, but the Darden Hills I'd never heard of except in the song we bellowed:

Charlie Chaplin, his shoes are crackin',
And his old baggy trousers, they want mending,
Before descending to the Darden Hills.

But I found out when I got older that the last line should have been—'*Before they send him to the Dardanelles*'.

With Bern and Bunt at work, Betty away in service and the rest of us at school, life began to be a little easier for our mother, and she gradually re-furnished the home by going to house sales, often picking up good bargains. She would career off on her old push-bike and come struggling home hours later with her purchases. Once she bought a carpet for five shillings—about fifty years old it was. 'Waste of good money,' our stepfather said when he saw the faded bundle.

'I can cut a lot of good bits out of that,' she told him. 'There's pieces in that carpet that's never seen daylight—been stuck under some sideboard for years—real Axminster it is—look—it's stamped on the back.' And she cut and joined the not-so-worn pieces together and made a carpet to cover our living-room.

Sometimes she would linger at the sales too long and come puffing down the road about half an hour before our stepfather was due in for tea. With her hat and coat on she would start cooking, with us children rushing about like mad things helping her. 'Quick Mollie—go and find some dry sticks to jostle the fire up and bring a shovel of little knobs of coal too.' Mick would be sent up the garden to pick sprouts, while she herself hurriedly peeled the potatoes, cutting the skins off thick and rough. For a while pandemonium raged.

'Ben,' Mother would shout, 'pop out to the gate and see if your father's coming,' and Ben would come rushing back crying:

'He's just up by the milkman's.'

'Then you and Denis get off up the road to meet him,' she'd yell. 'It'll give me an extra five minutes.'

Our stepfather would get off his bicycle and sit Ben on the saddle and Denis on the carrier and slowly walk the rest of the way home. When he finally got indoors all was calm. Our mother in a clean pinafore would just be in the act of pouring him out a cup of tea. Potatoes and sprouts in separate string nets would be boiling away on the

bright fire, and the home-cured bacon was sizzling in a pan on the hob.

She was generous to a fault, often giving away things we could do with ourselves. Once she gave a tramp half a bread pudding meant for our stepfather's tea. When he grumbled at her for it she said, 'Half of them aren't roaders, just poor devils who can't get work. Surely you don't begrudge them a mouthful of food.'

Next day one of the neighbours sent us a bucket of chitterlings as a gift. 'There you are!' she cried. 'Cast your bread upon the water and it'll come back to you with butter on.' And she rolled up her sleeves and set about cleaning the messy innards.

When there were smelly jobs to do, like chitterlings-cleaning or drawing the insides from rabbits and fowls, our mother used to sweeten the air indoors by burning a few sprigs of dried lavender. She would light the stalks and whirl them round and round, filling the room with a sweet summer smell. When our precious Axminster needed sweeping she would lay damp tea-leaves, straight from the tea-pot, onto the edge of the carpet and sweep them right across it to pick up the dust.

As we got older our mother did all she could to encourage us to broaden our outlook, and would cycle miles with us. We explored Roman Villas, churches in fields miles from anywhere, holy wells and ancient moats, cruck houses and old preaching crosses.

When we got back from these expeditions she would send us down to the lending library to get books on the things we had seen or on the locality. She taught us to find pleasure from simple country things—to appreciate sunsets and sunrises and each season in turn. To her, everything had a golden glow; even the common dandelion was a thing of beauty in her eyes.

209

I never see the sun breaking through the leaves without remembering the simple way she instilled in our minds that beauty was ours for the looking. I have heard her say that, after living in the same cottage for over fifteen years, she could still look out of the window and see something different every morning.

Walking back from Witney, sometimes with the east wind roaring against us, she would quote George Borrow's—'There's the wind on the heath, brother'. She never minded being out in all weathers; the only thing she objected to was fog—horrible and unhealthy was her opinion of it, and it blocked her vision of the outside world which she loved so much.

Much of her time in later years was spent 'catching up' on all the books she had not had time to read when we were small.

She taught us to respect our fellow men, saying, 'If you can't say anything good about anybody, don't say anything bad.'

And as each of us started work she gave us a bit of useful advice: 'Keep your job by working hard. Don't try to keep it by telling tales.'

One thing she never did was to tell anyone how old she was. And we children never dared ask her. But when friends and relations brought up the subject she would smilingly answer, 'As old as me tongue and a little bit older than me teeth,' which was perfectly true anyway. And when she died we found out that she was, in fact, eight years older than any of us had imagined.

A Time to Remember

BY the end of the 1920s a gradual change had come over all our lives. We older ones had begun to spread our wings like a brood of young fledglings, gradually breaking away from the old ways, leaving the elderly to sing at church and camp meetings.

Bern had saved hard and bought himself a fine racing bike. He joined the Oxford Cycling Club and on Sundays he would go along with dozens of other young men, smartly plus-foured, tearing through the countryside, heads down, behinds in the air. A hundred miles or more they would go sometimes! Bunt was courting strong and saving every penny so that he and his Sylvia could marry.

A TIME TO REMEMBER

Betty, fed up with service, had come back home to the crowded cottage and had got herself a job at a laundry in the town. She stood ironing all day long with a couple of dozen other girls. The work was hard but quite well paid, and they laughed and sang as they smoothed the creases from the gentry's clothes.

She went dancing on Saturday nights; she wore fancy garters, cami-knickers and French knickers, and curled her already wavy hair with a pair of curling tongs, thrusting them into the fire, then twirling her hair up with the hot irons to make it frizzy. She used lipstick, and strange boys used to wait outside our gate for her, sometimes coming on their push-bikes from other villages to see her. She was beautiful.

When I left school she 'spoke for me' at the laundry, asking Mrs. Cameron if she could find me a job. I was put in the sorting- and packing-room. For a while I had to walk backwards and forwards to work until our stepfather picked up a second-hand bicycle cheaply for me. But I was rather a misfit at the laundry: big and clumsy and a bit of a tom-boy. Mrs. Cameron used to swear at me and say, 'You'll never be the lady your sister is, why can't you behave nicely like Betty?' But my sister had the advantage over me—that year away in service had taught her a lot, whereas I had come raw, straight from a village school.

I stuck the job as long as I could. Our mother kept saying how lucky I was to be working at such a nice place, but it was no good. One bright Saturday morning the rebel in me surged up. Mrs. Cameron called me 'a black-headed bugger' for some trifling thing. I gave her a mouthful of cheek that for once left her speechless and ran out of the laundry—and got another job within the next hour.

It was around this time that Alice Spindlow and I used to pretend to go down to church on Sunday nights. Then we would slip back over 'The Moors' and up to Witney, to walk up and down The Causeway or 'Bunny Run' as some called it, in an effort to 'get off' with boys. One night Alice bought some liquorice allsorts. In them we found a nice round red one and we smeared the red all over our lips, trying in vain to look grown-up. 'They 'ad thur mouths made up, they looked as if they'd cut thur throats,' one of the villagers told our mother. And that put an end to our walking up the Bunny Run for a while.

As we lay lazily abed on summer mornings, loath to get up for work, we could hear Walter Weaver go plodding over 'The Moors' on his way to work. He always wore great heavy boots. His father was a farm labourer and they lived up in the fields somewhere. Walter had to walk down muddy lanes leading to Ducklington, then on to Witney, so heavy boots were essential. He had the steady gait of the ploughman following the furrow and he always sang loudly as he went—for weeks it was: 'I'm Goin' Back to 'im as 'as, 'im as 'as a Pub Next Door.' When he got tired of that one it was 'Tiptoe Through the Tulips' for weeks on end. Other tunes followed—'All by Yourself in the Moonlight', 'Springtime in the Rockies', and 'The Old Kitchen Kettle'.

Bet and I used to stay in bed until the last minute. With sleep still in our eyes we would stand and gulp down hot tea, our mother would shove our lunch into our hands, and then we were away up the town to work.

We began to join clothing clubs—The Great

Universal Stores was the favourite. By doing this we could order a new coat or shoes, and then it would take weeks to pay the bill.

The G.W.R. started to run cheap trips to the sea-side. You could go to Brighton or Southsea for about 4s 6d. When we could afford it some of us would go, taking sandwiches, enough for the day, for nobody had money to spend on food. We used to start eating them almost as soon as the train pulled out.

Soon boys began waiting outside the gate for me as well as for Betty; shy lads they were, too—sometimes bringing bunches of flowers with them, carefully tied on to the handlebars of their bicycles—violets and primroses, cowslips and dog roses. Some of the lads wore a great big buttonhole, as big as a saucer, in their lapels, and a nice swank handker-chief in their top pocket.

The lanes and fields that had been our playground for so long now became our courting places. I used to have dreadful crushes on some of these boys—for weeks I would have lain down and died for them; then suddenly it was off with the old and on with the new, until our mother thought that I would never take anyone seriously for any length of time. 'You're not bringing any more fellows home,' she would say, 'making fools of them—you'll go round the orchard and pick up a crab if you're not careful.'

In the village, too, things were changing. Mick

did not have to stay at Ducklington school until she was fourteen as we older ones did, but went along with the other kids of the village up to Witney for the last couple of years of her education.

Collis's bought a van to deliver their bread in. They also became owners of a couple of sleek black cars that were used for local weddings and funerals and general taxi-ing, with one of Mr. Collis's daughters doing the driving. Benny Clements, the old oil man, no longer came round on Saturdays. Hog Puddin' Walker and Spetter King passed away too.

Now each week on Fridays a pretty ginger-haired girl called, driving a green motor van. She sold all sorts of things to eat, including cold fried fish which our mother used to buy and warm up for our tea.

Betty found a cheap gramophone in Jacky Brooke's second-hand shop in the town and almost every week she bought a new record—songs by Layton and Johnston, Hutch, and Gracie Fields.

The talkies came to The People's Palace at Witney and we began to use slang expressions like 'Sez You', 'Oh Yeah' and 'Sez Me', as the great spectaculars flashed across the screen. Waites' ha'p'nny leg dangle paid their annual visit to the town but hardly anyone went—the talkies were much more exciting and we never heard of the Waites travelling theatre again.

Times were changing even faster now. Boys came a-courting us on motor-bikes and in cars. We went dancing night after night—sometimes to real big dances, Police Balls, Fat-Stock Dances with red-faced farmers for partners—Twelfth Night and the annual Conservative Ball.

Bet and I made most of our own dance dresses, running them up on the old hand sewing-machine. One day our mother went to a jumble sale in the village, bringing back a most lovely dance dress which she had bought for one shilling. Flame georgette it was, with a fringe of real fine ostrich feathers round the bottom. Betty looked like a Queen in it. 'I shall wear it to the Corn Exchange Dance tonight,' she said, ripping off the lovely ostrich feather fringe.

'But that makes the dress,' Mother protested.

'And how do you think I can explain such luxury to the laundry girls?' Betty cried. 'I shall go up to Witney and buy a bit of lampshade fringe from Georgie Wickham's and sew it on in place of the feathers and then they'll think I made it myself.'

'I see the Witney Ladies' Hockey Club want some new members,' Mother said to me one day. 'Why don't you join? Funny,' she went on, 'I saw a second-hand hockey stick in the town yesterday, 'twas only three and six!'

So, without knowing one end of a hockey stick from another, I joined the club, greenly explaining that I could not play. One of the older members took me to her home, and after telling me how the game was played, taught me all the rules—she even had to tell me how to hold the stick! I stayed with the Club for years. Mick joined later.

We took up tennis and continued to swim in the Windrush from the first of May till the end of September, and all the time thoroughly enjoying ourselves, although we were always perpetually hard up.

Our stepfather bought a series of old motorcycles—he was clever with engines, and soon had them ticking over like new. He used to go off early some Sunday mornings to see his ageing Mother, often taking one of his children on the pillion. Other Sundays his brothers and sisters used to visit us. They came on motor-bikes, too—great roaring things they were.

Bunt and Sylvia got married and Bet and I were bridesmaids for the first and last time in our lives.

It was around this time that we moved from 'Wayside' to a new bungalow about a mile away from Ducklington, but well outside the town. For our mother, especially, the move must have been wonderful after the crowded years at Wayside. At last we girls had a bedroom of our own, instead of sharing a curtained-off one with our brothers. We had a wardrobe and a drawer each, in a newly acquired chest of drawers.

Bern, Ben and Denis shared a second bedroom and our parents the other. We had a front room (for courting), a living-room, kitchen and bathroom.

Water was pumped from a spring by a rotary pump and was heated in the copper in the kitchen, and the bath-water had to be carried through into the bathroom, but at least the water ran away on its own into a cesspool in the huge garden. The lavatory, too, was indoors but we still used oil lamps and candles for lighting.

A TIME TO REMEMBER

We had a summer-house and a greenhouse, and kept pigs and chickens and bees.

But I missed the cosiness of the cottage and the nearness of the big family, and I longed to return to the crowded living-room at Wayside and the cheese box under the bed where I kept my few clothes.

I became restless, walking for miles on my own. I fell out with my boy friends and began to write both poetry and prose. As I walked along the twisty leafy lanes I knew that the magic of my youth was gradually fading away. The funny, familiar things that had happened during those green years were already half-forgotten memories. I was trying desperately to hang on to a world that would never come back again, but it was months before I realised this.

The writing became less now—my sisters teased the life out of me about it, anyhow. But one poem, the only one that finally emerged from that time, and yet was not completed until after our mother died, explains the heartbreak on leaving the cottage at Ducklington.

Wild roses of my home,
you climb and circle round my brain,
stirring my aching heart
with your festooned loveliness,
taunting me with your delicate perfume.

Let me return
to those sun-drenched lanes
to press my face
in your bee-kissed blossom,
brush my cheek
as the gentle breeze
loosens your pale blooms,
spilling your fragrance
over the dew-wet grass,
speckling my path
with confettied profusion,
your thorns
stabbing the memory,
flooding the mind's pool
with nostalgic dreams
of half-forgotten childhood.

Let me return
where the wild rose blooms,
drowning my empty heart
in your summer glory,
cooling my fevered brow
in the lost fields of home.

Note

Parts of this book have already appeared in different form, in broadcasts by the B.B.C., and as articles in the *Witney Gazette*, the *Oxfordshire Roundabout*, and the *Oxford Times*.